*For help with family problems,
for confidence in making decisions,
for comfort in times of need . . .*

"Catherine Marshall reminds Christians that reliance on the Holy Spirit is essential. Each chapter gives evidence of people overcoming dire tragedies with the help of prayers to the Holy Ghost. Some are awesome, documented cases of miraculous cures, others are instances of regained faith and all are fascinating. . . . She writes unassumingly, simply and with palpable sincerity."
Publishers Weekly

"Catherine Marshall is one of America's finest Christian writers. . . . The book is dotted with evidence of her beautiful gift of painting word pictures. . . . The short devotional studies are carefully laid out, and thoughtfully presented. . . . It provides clear insights, simply set forth for those seeking a closer relationship with God, the Holy Spirit. . . . Penetrating and provocative . . . this book will beautifully guide."
Contemporary Christian Acts

Other Avon Books by
Catherine Marshall

BEYOND OURSELVES
CATHERINE MARSHALL'S STORY BIBLE
CHRISTY
JULIE
A MAN CALLED PETER
SOMETHING MORE
TO LIVE AGAIN

CATHERINE MARSHALL

The Helper

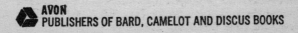

AVON
PUBLISHERS OF BARD, CAMELOT AND DISCUS BOOKS

Scripture quotations identified MOFFATT are from *The Bible: A New Translation* by James Moffatt. Copyright 1954 by James A. R. Moffatt. By permission of Harper & Row, Publishers, Inc.

Scripture quotations identified RSV are from The Revised Standard Version of the Bible, copyright 1946, 1952, © 1971, 1973 by the Division of Christian Education of the National Council of the Churches of Christ in the U.S.A., and used by permission.

Scripture quotations identified KJV are from the King James Version of the Bible.

Scripture quotations identified NEB are from the New English Bible © The Delegates of the Oxford University Press and the Syndics of the Cambridge University Press 1961 and 1970. Reprinted by permission.

Old Testament Scripture quotations identified AMPLIFIED are from *Amplified Bible, Old Testament*, copyright 1962, 1964 by Zondervan Publishing House, and are used by permission.

New Testament Scripture quotations identified AMPLIFIED are from the Amplified New Testament © The Lockman Foundation 1958, and are used by permission.

AVON BOOKS
A division of
The Hearst Corporation
1790 Broadway
New York, New York 10019

Copyright © 1978 by Catherine Marshall
Published by arrangement with Chosen Books Publishing Co., Ltd.
Library of Congress Catalog Card Number: 77-15875
ISBN: 0-380-45583-8

First Avon Printing, December 1979

AVON TRADEMARK REG. U.S. PAT. OFF. AND IN
OTHER COUNTRIES, MARCA REGISTRADA,
HECHO EN U.S.A.

Printed in the U.S.A.

OPM   15   14   13   12   11   10   9

To
my son Peter
and to
Edith,
the daughter God gave me

Acknowledgments

I wish to express my appreciation to my secretaries, Jeanne Sevigny and Jean Brown, who as usual have patiently typed and retyped their way through the various versions of this manuscript; to Ruth McWilliams for her assistance in research and in copy-editing; for the special typing help of Louise Gibbons.

My special gratitude to my husband Leonard LeSourd, always an exacting critic and reliable sounding board; and to the close friends in both our Florida and Virginia fellowship groups, with whom I have shared the discoveries about the Helper recorded in these pages and the day-by-day living out of those discoveries.

C. M.

Contents

Foreword

In the early summer of 1944 I found myself curious about what seemed a strange subject indeed—the Holy Ghost. It was not that I had heard any sermon on this topic, or read a book, or been a part of some lively discussion group. Indeed, nothing overt had happened to spark this curiosity. It was rather as if I were hearing for the first time a replay of a lifetime of ecclesiastical garnishes that had hitherto floated past me—the endings of prayers, benedictions, christenings, communions, weddings and the like using the term "Holy Ghost" or "Holy Spirit." An inner spotlight now focused on this. Questions nagged and would not be silenced. . . . What was so significant about this spooky-sounding term? Why had the Church clung tenaciously to something seemingly so archaic? In short, what was this all about?

With the perspective of the years, I now know that God Himself had carefully planted the curiosity in me. For it was no passing whim. It did not go away, and it had ample emotional, intellectual, and volitional energy fueling it to keep me at a summer-long quest for answers to my questions.

I decided to go to the one place I could count on for final authoritative truth—the Bible. Scripture had never yet deceived me or led me astray. From long experience I knew that the well-worn words from an old church ordinance had it exactly right—the Bible still is "the only infallible rule of faith and practice."

At the same time I also knew that the search in Scripture could be no random dipping in; it had to be thorough and

11

all-inclusive. A Bible, a Cruden's Concordance, a loose-leaf notebook, pen, and colored pencils were my only tools.

All summer I gave a minimum of an hour a day to this. Using the various terms referring to the third Person of the Trinity, I looked up every reference in the Concordance, Old and New Testament. Morning by morning revealed new truths—new to me at least. Such as that in Old Testament times only certain prophets, priests, and kings were given the Spirit. Even then, the Spirit was given them only "by measure"—that is, a partial giving. So that was why Joel's prophecy,[1] fulfilled at Pentecost, was such startling news: in that great day the Spirit for the first time in history became available to *all* flesh, no longer "by measure" but in His fullness!

Or on another morning I discovered that John the Baptist, as the forerunner of Christ, was granted a unique gift—the Spirit from birth.[2] Jesus on the other hand, did not receive the baptism of the Spirit until He was about thirty years old at the time John baptized Him in the Jordan. Up to that time, Christ had performed no miracles or "mighty works." So even the Son of God Himself did not dare begin His public ministry without the power of the Spirit.

The messages kept piling up. I discovered that the fullness of the Holy Spirit is *not* something that happens automatically at conversion. His coming to us and living within us is a gift, the best gift the Father can give us. But the Father always waits on our volition. Jesus told us that we have to desire this gift, ask for it—ask for Him.

Something else shimmered through too. It's the Spirit who is the Miracle-Worker. When our churches ignore Him, no wonder they are so devoid of answered prayer. No wonder they have rationalized and developed an unscriptural position: the belief that miracles were only for the beginning years of the faith to get the Church started!

Rather, the truth is that Scripture assumes miracles. And the Helper (one of the names Jesus gave the Holy Spirit) always brings miracles in His wake, moves in the climate of miracles, expects them.

By now I was excited. I was also increasingly incredulous about the silence of the churches on this subject. How was it that I could not recall ever hearing a sermon on the Holy Spirit? Why was this not taught in Sunday School?

Naturally, I did not keep quiet about the search I was

on. My enthusiasm for my mounting discoveries was shared with Peter Marshall. It was happily inevitable that the study had to spill over into life. We asked for the great gift of the Spirit. Very quietly, by faith, we received Him— with immense richness and blessing added to our lives. The blessings have followed across the years and, for me, the unfolding joy of ever-new learning is still going on.

That was how, during the last years of Peter Marshall's life, two strong strands of teaching emerged in his ministry —a greater emphasis than ever on healing through prayer, and the beginning of an emphasis on the Holy Spirit. The healing renewal in the Church had begun in the Anglican Church in England and was at that time beginning to be reflected in Episcopal circles in America. But so far as Peter and I knew, there was no one who shared our new-found enthusiasm for the Holy Spirit's mission in our contemporary world. After all, this was twenty years before the tremendous revival of interest in the subject in the sixties.

Then in 1945 the editor of the Presbyterian monthly devotional magazine *Today* asked Peter to author an issue. Up to that time, each issue had been a miscellany of thirty or thirty-one assorted topics. Peter suggested to the editor that he and I coauthor the devotionals, and that they be the study of a single topic for the month. The editor agreed. The topic Peter and I chose was the Holy Spirit.

The resultant July 1945 issue of *Today* met with a surprising response. Copies were quickly exhausted, with readers writing in for more copies. In the next two or three years this issue was reprinted once, then again. As late as 1954 *Today*'s editor was writing in "The Editor's Visit" in the front of the April issue:

> Requests for back issues of *Today* on "The Holy Spirit," written by the Marshalls, keep coming to the Editor's office, but he is sorry to report that the supply is completely exhausted.

Those 1945 devotionals taken from the original summer-long study form the core of the material that follows. Since the Holy Spirit must and ever will be our Teacher, to that first material I have added more of His teaching and the insights He has given in the years since.

Back in 1945 Peter and I could never have foreseen the

amazing resurgence of the Spirit that began early in the sixties and by 1966-67 was in full swing. By ten years later, at least 500,000 members of mainline Protestant churches and 2,000,000 Catholics were involved in this renewal. Books on the subject began flooding from the presses.

Even with all this interest in the Holy Spirit, many church members are still wondering (just as I did back in 1944) whether this is another religious fad that will fade like all other fads. And whether its proponents are odd, eccentric people, just another brand of fanatics? Finally, whether this Helper can have any important bearing on his or her life?

If such wonderings are more than a passing vagary, the inquirer then speculates about where he can get reliable information about the Spirit. To such a seeker, I could give no better reply than that Dr. A. B. Simpson gave to some inquirers about the gospel of healing back in 1915:

> I sent them to their homes to read God's Word for themselves and ponder and pray . . . [because one must be] fully persuaded of the Word of God in this matter. This is the only sure foundation of rational and Scriptural faith. Your faith must rest on the great principles and promises of the Bible, or it never can stand the testing of the oppositions and trials that are sure to come. You must be so sure that this is part of the gospel and the redemption of Christ that all the teachings and reasonings of the best of men cannot shake you. . . .[3]

Dr. Simpson's advice is as sound and applicable to the baptism of the Spirit as to healing. The purpose then of the devotionals that follow is to go back to Scripture to discover what it would teach us about the Helper. Let the Bible speak to you where you are. You can trust it. Have no fear about resting your whole weight and, indeed, your very life on its message.

It is a shining promised land into which the Holy Spirit would lead all of us, that land prepared for the heirs—the beloved sons and daughters of the King. We do not have to wait for death to enter. It is for the here and now.

But the promised land won't come to us. Our entering in is volitional: it is necessary that we make up our minds and our wills to rise and enter.

When we do, the promise is sure,

Every place that the sole of your foot shall tread upon, that have I given unto you. . . .[4] *Joshua 1:3*

No wonder the gospel is "glad tidings of great joy to all men!"

Catherine Marshall

Evergreen Farm, Virginia
October 5, 1977

How to Use This Book

Since the Helper can never be packaged or programmed to fit any man-devised plan, the way to approach this book is with open expectancy. It has been written out of my own spiritual need to speak to those who share my longing for thirst-quenching quaffs of the Living Water.

The forty "helps," of course, are ideal for the forty days of Lent as a devotional guide—either for individuals or for study groups. But *The Helper* is also a book for all seasons just as the power of the Holy Spirit is needed every day of the year to help us cope with the problems and complexities of the difficult times we are living in.

For individual use, I recommend setting aside the same time each day, in the same quiet place, for reading, checking Bible references, and personal prayer. It helps to be very specific in one's prayer requests. This can become an exciting experiment by the keeping of a Prayer Log in which each petition is jotted down by date, with space left to record the date of the answer as well as details about how it came.

The little feature *His Word for You* at the end of each Help came from all the Scripture promises I began copying in a notebook about two years ago. This is the rationale that led me to begin searching out the promises . . .

If one of us were notified that a wealthy man had included us in his will, we would be eager to know what that man's "last will and testament" said.

It is not by chance that the word testament is used in Scripture—Old *Testament* . . . New *Testament*.

Our Father is very wealthy. And the news is out; the richest One in the universe has designated us among His heirs. How eagerly we should be searching His will and testament to find out exactly what it is He has bequeathed us.

Anyone's inheritance always comes first in the form of a statement of intent, some promises on a piece of paper. Our inheritance from the Father follows the same order. Some of these promises have conditions attached, some do not. When we meet the condition, then the promise becomes a prophecy of what will come about. So it would be accurate to think of *His Word for You* as your personal word of prophecy, something to anticipate with greatest joy.

What a treasure these promises are! With the door of the treasure house open to us, why should we remain hungry paupers when we are heirs of the Father and joint-heirs with the Father's only-begotten, beloved Son!

Step out then to claim joyously each one of your bequests.

C. M.

Part One

Introducing
the Helper

1 *Who Is the Helper?*

*And I will ask the Father, and He will give you another
. . . Helper . . . that He may remain with you forever.*

*. . . . you know and recognize Him, for He lives with you
[constantly] and will be in you.*
                    (John 14:16, 17, AMPLIFIED)

Most of us begin by thinking of the Holy Spirit as an
influence, something ghostly, floating, ethereal that pro-
duces a warm and loving feeling in us. We betray this
misconception by using the impersonal pronoun "it" when
speaking of the Spirit.

But the Helper is no influence; He is rather a Person—
one of the three Persons of the Godhead. As such, He
possesses all the attributes of personality. He has a mind;[1]
He has knowledge;[2] He has a will.[3]   I Co. 12:11   Ro. 8:12

In addition, the Spirit acts and forms relationships only
possible with a person. Check for yourself these texts:

I Co. 2:10,11

He speaks (Acts 1:16) Spoke Thru David {Ps 69:25 / Ps 109:8}
He prays (Romans 8:26,27)
He teaches (John 14:26)
He works miracles (Acts 2:4; 8:39)
He can be resisted (Acts 7:51)— Stubborn
He commands (Acts 8:29; 11:12; 13:2)
He forbids (Acts 16:6,7)

The Helper's work on earth today is also to administrate
the Church, Christ's body on earth. For instance, He sets

ministers over churches.[4] He distributes varying gifts and ministries to individual members of the Church,[5] and so on.

To crown all this, the Spirit, being a Person, is a Friend whom we can come to know and to love. One of His most lovable characteristics is that He deliberately submerges Himself in Jesus; He works at being inconspicuous.

This was illustrated recently at a banquet honoring a woman retiring from twenty-five years as head of the Sunday School Beginner's Department. Patiently, without self-consciousness, she had endured the speeches praising her.

Then she rose to speak. In three minutes, as the Spirit spoke through her, she preached one of the most eloquent sermons we had ever heard . . .

"All these years," she told us, "the children have been teaching me about Jesus. He's real to them, and they have made Him more real to me than I would have thought possible twenty-five years ago."

Her eyes were twinkling. "For instance, I remember the little boy who burst out with, 'If Jesus came right through that door now, I'd run right up and hug Him.'

"I owe such a great deal to the children. . . ."

As she sat down, we no longer thought of her—only of Jesus.

And that is typical of the Helper. Always there is a transparency in His personality so that Jesus can shine through. It is the Spirit's specific work to reveal facets of the Lord's personality rather than His own to us; to woo us and lead us to that Other, to glorify Him, to bring *Him* and *His* words to our remembrance.[6]

There are those who wonder whether the present-day movement of the Spirit may not be placing too great an emphasis on this Third Person of the Trinity. We need not be troubled about that. For the Helper always sees to it that He acts as a spotlight, ever focused on Jesus, so that we are not aware of the spotlight itself, only of that One who stands bathed in the brilliant illumination.

Thus an authentic hallmark of the believer baptized in the Spirit is that Jesus as a living Person becomes more real to him than ever before. That is the Spirit's glorious gift to you and me.

HELPFUL READING: John 16:7-31

HIS WORD FOR YOU: He is eager to answer us.

And it shall be that before they call I will answer, and while they are yet speaking I will hear.

(Isaiah 65:24, AMPLIFIED)

PRAYER: *Lord, I need the Helper today because I need to have the greatest gift of all, that You become real to me. There is not a single part of my life where I do not need Your help, Lord Jesus. Forgive me for those days when I haven't taken the time to talk things over with You. When I ignore You, I am the loser. Sometimes I tell myself that I am too busy to pray. That is self-deception. The truth is that I have a strange resistance to face You and to be honest with You. Lord, I give You permission to melt that resistance.*

Today I ask the Helper to nudge me into using the day's chinks of time to pray—when I'm driving or walking, or standing in line for something, or waiting my turn in the dentist's or doctor's office. So help me to practice Your Presence, Lord. Amen.

2 *Why Do I Need the Helper?*

But you shall receive power when the Holy Spirit has come upon you; and you shall be my witness in Jerusalem and in all Judea and Samaria and to the end of the earth.

(Acts 1:8, RSV)

Jesus was about thirty years old when He asked John the Baptist to baptize Him. Behind Him lay "the hidden years" of which we catch only glimpses in the Gospels. We do know that until then He had lived a quiet life in the Nazareth carpenter shop and had attempted "no mighty works."

That day at the Jordan the Holy Spirit came upon Him, permanently to make His home in the earthly temple of Christ's being. Only then did Jesus dare to embark on His public ministry.

In the same way, three years later the disciples were instructed by their Master not to attempt to preach or to teach or to witness until this same heavenly Dove had implanted His fire in their hearts too . . .

He commanded them not to leave Jerusalem, but to wait for what the Father had promised. . . .[1] Acts 1:4

Only the Holy Spirit could give them the ability to communicate truth to other people; could supply them with in-depth perception into the needs of others; could give them a message; convict of sin; heal; administer the infant Church—in short, equip them for service.

We in our century are certainly no less needy than our

24

Lord or those first disciples. For us to attempt any church work, any ministry or witnessing solely through man's devices, talents, and organizational machinery alone is as effective as trying to drive our car with water in the gasoline.

The year 1871 saw Dwight L. Moody apparently a great success as an evangelist. His tabernacle drew the largest congregations in Chicago. But according to Moody's own estimate of those years, he was "a great hustler" and this work was being done "largely in the energy of the flesh."[2]

Two humble Free Methodist women, Auntie Cook and Mrs. Snow, used to attend these meetings and sit on the front row. Moody could not help seeing that they were praying during most of his services. Finally he spoke to the women about it.

"Yes," they admitted, "we have been praying for you."

"Why me? Why not for the unsaved?" the evangelist retorted, a bit nettled.

"Because you need the power of the Spirit," was their answer.

After some weeks of this Mr. Moody invited the women to his office to talk about it. "You spoke of power for service," he prodded them. "I thought I had it. I wish you would tell me what you mean."

So Mrs. Snow and Auntie Cook told Moody what they knew about the baptism of the Holy Spirit. Then the three Christians prayed together—and the women left.

From that hour "there came a great hunger in my soul," Moody was to say later. "I really felt that I did not want to live if I could not have this power for service."

One late autumn day in 1871 Dwight L. Moody was in New York (on his way to England) walking up Wall Street. Suddenly, in the midst of the bustling crowds, his prayer was answered: the power of God fell on him so overwhelmingly that he knew he must get off the street.

Spotting a house he recognized, Moody knocked on the door and asked if he might have a room by himself for a few hours. Alone there, such joy came upon him that "at last he had to ask God to withhold His hand, lest he die on the spot from very joy."

From that hour Moody's ministry was never the same. He went on to England for what was to be the first of many evangelistic campaigns there. People thronged to North London to hear him.

"The sermons were not different," Moody summarized. "I did not present any new truths, and yet hundreds were converted. I would not now be placed back where I was before that blessed experience if you should give me all the world."

The evangelist was to live another twenty-eight years, and "to reduce the population of hell by a million souls." Through the Moody Bible Institute, the Moody Press, the Northfield Conferences, the Northfield and Mt. Hermon Schools, the vigor and power of his work continues to this day.

HELPFUL READING: ACTS 1:1–14

HIS WORD FOR YOU: He is out ahead opening the way. *Behold I am doing a new thing; now it springs forth; do you not perceive and know it, and will you not give heed to it? I will even make a way in the wilderness and rivers in the desert.*

(Isaiah 43:19, AMPLIFIED)

PRAYER: *Lord, there are members of my family and friends who are hurting. They need You so sorely. Yet I don't know how to tell them the good news that You really are alive, that You love them, that help is available.*

Lord, I see that there is no way to get through to them unless You give me this gift of Your Spirit for service. I know that this is a "dangerous" prayer, but I ask you to create a hunger for that explosion of joy and love in my heart too. And I thank You for the sure promise that all of us who hunger and thirst for righteousness "shall be filled."[3] In Thy Name. Amen.

Mt 5:6

3 Have I Already Received Him?

And he said, "Into what then were you baptized?" They said, "Into John's baptism."

(Acts 19:3, RSV)

Paul was asking this question of the believers at Ephesus about twenty years after Pentecost. He made one thing very clear to these believers. He expected them to know the difference between John's baptism and Jesus' baptism.

The Ephesians' answer: "We have experienced only John's baptism." This meant that they had repented and received the forgiveness of their sins, but that they understood nothing about Jesus' enabling power for handling life in the present and the future.

So what was "John's baptism"? John the Baptist was the last of the Old Testament prophets. With John the era of the Old Testament closed forever. It had been a long dry period of the dispensation of law, with men trying to bridge the estrangement between them and the holy, just Jehovah by repentance, by obeying a multiplicity of laws, and by good works. The law could point men to the ideal,[1] but lacked power to help men keep the laws or to change character.

In crisp terms Jesus Himself assessed John the Baptist and the era just closing for us:

Truly, I tell you, among those born of women there has not risen one greater than John the Baptist; yet he

27

who is least in the kingdom of heaven is greater than he.[2] Mt: 11:11

"John is a great man, the greatest," Jesus was saying. "Yet the humblest disciple in the kingdom I am here to inaugurate has riches and privileges and graces, yes, and authority of which John never dreamed."

How could that be? Because man's efforts—even his best efforts—were at an end. In the new era of the kingdom, it would be God's Spirit *in* man doing the work.

So Paul sought to lead those Ephesian believers out of that Old Testament era of human striving into the glorious kingdom of the Risen One.

"Into what were you baptized?" is as pertinent a question today. It has prompted me to some sharp self-examination:

First, have I ever asked God for this gift, for Jesus' baptism of the Spirit, and claimed, by faith, Christ's promise?[3] Lk 11:13

Have I any evidence of the Holy Spirit's work in my life? For instance, has the Spirit made Jesus real to me as a Person?[4] Jn. 15:26

Am I beginning to be able to hear the inner Voice of the Spirit? Does He tell me what to do for small decisions or major ones?[5] Ro. 8:14

Am I seeing in myself a new kind of love for other people? Is the Spirit giving me a tender concern and deep caring for persons whom I would ordinarily not choose as my friends?[6] Ga 5:22   James 2:8 9

Am I experiencing the Spirit's help in the always tricky area of communication? For instance, am I experiencing times when the Helper gives my words wings into the heart of someone in trouble?

Am I experiencing the power of the Spirit? For example, to communicate Jesus' life to others, to bring them also into the kingdom?

Am I receiving the Spirit's definite help in how to pray about my deepest concerns?[7] Ro. 8:26

These are some of the strands of the Helper's work in the lives He fills. Am I, like the Ephesians, a stranger to His work?

HELPFUL READING: Luke 7:19–35

HIS WORD FOR YOU: Our Savior-King.

> *For the Lord is our judge,*
> *the Lord is our law-giver,*
> *the Lord is our king;*
> *He will save us.*
>
>   (Isaiah 33:22, AMPLIFIED)

PRAYER: *Lord, I would not indulge in the kind of spiritual analysis that is still self-centered. Yet I know that Your truth means definiteness and clarity. The fuzziness that I've sometimes mistakenly taken for spirituality is part of my humanness, not Your Divine Order. I know that Your truth and Your life in me will mean real and noticeable progress.*

Lord, I need to have You lift my everyday life to another level altogether. I not only give You permission, but ask You to make in me whatever changes are necessary to receive Your Spirit. Amen.

4 No Need to Be an Orphaned Christian

"I will not leave you orphans."
(John 14:18, Swedish Translation)

An orphan is one who has known the warmth of a father's and mother's love, the security of home and hearthside, and is then deprived of these gifts.

Jesus' apostles were fearful of being in exactly that position. For three years the Master had been everything to them—beloved Companion, staunch Friend, never-failing Guide, provocative, exciting Teacher. When they wanted to know how to pray with results, they had but to ask Him. When Peter daringly tried to walk on the water, then became fearful and began to sink, he had but to stretch out his hand to have Jesus rescue him.

But lately, more and more often their Master had been speaking of His own death. "The time is at hand," He now told them. With dismay the apostles heard His soft "I go away."

Then Jesus, seeing their anxious faces, noting Peter's fearful question, "Lord, I don't understand. Where are you going?" hastened to reassure them. "I will not leave you orphans," He promised the little group. "I will *not* leave you comfortless. I *will* manifest Myself to you."

So Jesus was telling His followers, "Look, having broken into the time-space capsule of Planet Earth and lived for a time among you, you don't think I'm going to leave you there, do you? For in that case, what would those have who come after you? Only the written record of Me as an historical figure. No contemporary expression of God, the

Father, or of Me—Jesus—for themselves. No, I won't leave it that way. I *will* come to you in the form of One who loves you as I do and is able to care for you even as I do now."

So it was that the apostles were about to enter a new period in history—the era of the Holy Spirit, the third Person of the Trinity, after God, the Father, and Jesus, the Son. This is the era that you and I are living in today.

It's no good our looking with longing to the Pre-Pentecost time of Jesus' days of public ministry on earth and trying to pretend that we are all still living in that other era. That would be wishful thinking and what's worse, delusion—living in unreality. But we do not need to look backwards. What Jesus has provided for us today, in our time, through the Helper is so much better.[1] Jn. 16:7

Jesus' promise to you and me is that the Helper will be with us always, day and night, standing by for any protection we need and for every emergency. Our only part is to recognize His presence and to call upon Him in joyous faith.

Once the truth of this amazing comradeship gets firmly imbedded in our mind and heart, we need never be afraid again, or lonely, or hopeless, or sorrowful, or helplessly inadequate. For the Helper is always with us, and altogether adequate.

Perhaps it would help us to understand if we place the Spirit's ministry in earth's time and space . . .

First Age	*Second Age*	*Third Age*
God, the Father.	God, the Son.	God, the Holy Spirit.
The law supreme.	Under grace.	Under election (a called-out people)
God spoke through a few prophets, priests, and kings.	Jesus teaching, healing, dying, rising again, glorified.	The restoration of a lost and defective world.
		The Holy Spirit sanctifies and works through the Church, Christ's Body.

Because the Holy Spirit is today present in His office on earth, all spiritual presence and divine communication of the Trinity with men are via the Spirit. In other words, while God, the Father, and God, the Son, are present and reigning in heaven, they are invisibly here in the body of the believer by the indwelling God, the Holy Spirit—the Helper.

Yet so long as we are ignorant of the Helper and His work, He cannot be fully operative in our lives. No wonder there is such vagueness and confusion in our minds when we speak or think of the Holy Spirit!

We have no greater need today than to be informed about the Helper. We need to know who He is, why we need Him, what He longs to do for us and our families, for our churches, and how we go about receiving Him. Otherwise we remain orphaned Christians—bereft of His love and of the magnificent fellowship, guidance and help He can give us.

HELPFUL READING: John 14:15–24

HIS WORD FOR YOU: He will direct our way.
And thine ears shall hear a word behind thee, saying, This is the way, walk ye in it, when ye turn to the right hand, and when ye turn to the left.
(Isaiah 30:21, KJV)

PRAYER: *"Jesus, without Thee we're orphaned and lonely,*
Come as our Teacher and Guide.
Leave us not comfortless, send us the Comforter,
Come to our hearts to abide."[8]

5 *Could Anything Be Better Than His Presence?*

It is to your advantage that I go away, for if I do not go away, the Counselor will not come for you; but if I go, I will send him to you.

(John 16:7, RSV)

How often we have envied those who saw Jesus in the flesh, who talked to Him and touched Him! Sometimes in the midst of some personal crisis we have thought wistfully, "If only I could hear His voice right now!"

It is the longing expressed so memorably in that classic children's hymn:

I wish that His hands had been placed on my head,
That His arms had been thrown around me,
And that I might have seen His kind look when He said,
"Let the little ones come unto Me!"[1]

We wonder how anything could be more wonderful than the physical presence of our Lord. Yet Jesus never spoke lightly or thoughtlessly. And here we have His solemn word in His Last Supper talk with His apostles that there *is* something better—His presence in the form of the Holy Spirit.

Moreover, in telling us this, Jesus used very practical businesslike terminology: it would be "expedient" for us, and to our calculated advantage, He said. What did He mean?

...vious fact that while Jesus
...to the fleshly limitations of
...who managed to get within
...only a few thousand at most
...His voice.

...e Helper, a new era would be
...ld Testament times up to the
...foretelling in this Last Supper
...came upon only a few chosen
...hem from above and without,
working ... inwardly.

In the new ... s telling us, His glorified presence
and His own resurrected life would be not only with us
but also *in* us,[2] progressively to transform us and our lives,
working from the inside outwardly.

As the Apostle John would later describe it:

> God's nature abides in him [us] . . . the divine sperm
> remains permanently within him. . . .[3]

This is the final outworking of that great Old Testament
promise:

> I will put my law in their inward parts, and write it
> in their hearts. . . .[4]

Here is a great mystery, difficult to put into words. It
becomes real and practical to us only as we walk it out.

Even in our time, we can observe two groups of Christians—those who have Christ beside them, *with* them, and
those who have the Lord Jesus *in them.*

The first group of Christians must still handle the knotty
problems of their lives on their own strength, with Jesus'
help. They get much help, of course, for a loving Lord will
always give us all we allow Him to give. So that's good, yet
not good enough.

The second group knows that they are as helpless as
Jesus said.[5] They also know that the "vine life" is the only
one that is going to bring heaven's power to earth and get
results: their life has to be inside the vine, an integral part
of its very cells and its life flow.[6] This inside life is what
the Spirit makes possible to us.

Recently, after a meeting where Jesus' teaching on this
had been explained, an Episcopal rector's wife approached

the visiting speaker. "I've been in the Church all my life," she said. "The vast difference between Jesus being *beside* us and His being *in us* had never even occurred to me. I *see it*! Light is bursting in all over!"

Now we begin to understand why Jesus said that the Helper's coming would be to our advantage. How we have underestimated and ignored this amazing blessing!

HELPFUL READING: John 14:15–17, 25–31

HIS WORD FOR YOU: Our faithful promise-keeping God.
And now, O Lord God, You are God and Your words are truth, and You have promised this good thing to Your servant.
(II Samuel 7:28, AMPLIFIED)

PRAYER: *Dear Jesus, I begin to see that the Holy Spirit has been more a pious term to me than the great reality You intended Him to be. It staggers me to think that He is more wonderful than Your physical presence would be. Yet this is Your own solemn estimate of the Helper's worth.*

I also begin to see, Lord, that since the Helper is really Your presence in another form, what You were telling Your apostles—and me—is that You Yourself will be in me.

This is almost too momentous for me to grasp, Lord. That Divinity would deign to dwell in my poor humanity!

One thing I do know, Lord. My heart needs to be cleansed and set in order for such a royal Guest. I give You permission now to prepare my inner being. And Lord, help me to be open and receptive. Amen.

6 *The Explosion of Power*

A new spirit will I put within you. . . .
And I will put my Spirit within you. . . .
        (Ezekiel 36:26, 27, AMPLIFIED)

Christianity was born into a world of trouble. The Roman world of the first century was awash in a rising tide of demoralization and evil. Today, we can see thought-provoking parallels between the period of the decline of the Roman Empire and our own time.

After His resurrection in many appearances, Jesus made it plain to His disciples that they were going to need His power to cope in such a disintegrating society. Therefore He instructed them to wait in Jerusalem until the Spirit came upon them.[1] Acts 1:1-5

The result was the explosion of power recorded in the first few chapters of the Acts. This first Pentecostal outpouring of God's Spirit was then to be followed by other explosions of power across the centuries. Always these have come when evil was rampant, when men and women were depressed and in spirit-bondage, when the fires of faith burned low.

The twelfth century saw such a rekindling of the fire of the Spirit under St. Francis of Assisi. For forty years these fires burned brightly in Italy.

Then, when the Mother Church was in a period of particular decadence, the monk Martin Luther nailed his ninety-five theses to the church door at Wittenburg. Who could have guessed that such a tiny spark could have kindled the conflagration of the Protestant Reformation of the sixteenth century!

Other outpourings of the Spirit have followed: the Evangelical quickening of the eighteenth century led by John and Charles Wesley; the Great Awakening in the American Colonies of the same period; the American Pentecostal revival of 1900–1905 that began in Topeka, Kansas, then spread to Los Angeles, California, where it made forever famous the address 312 Azusa Street; the South Wales revival of 1904–1905 for which the Spirit used the twenty-six-year-old layman Evan Roberts.

Those who have studied in detail these intermittent outpourings of the Spirit since Pentecost tell us that all have certain elements in common . . . *"Revivals, Their Laws and Leaders" by James Burns*

Nearly all have originated with the common people at a grass-roots level, outside the established church. The ever-present emphasis on repentance has usually drawn active, often bitter hostility from the Church.

All are characterized by a simplifying of the gospel and a return to Jesus Christ.

There is inevitably a great outpouring of joy and love.

Music always plays a large part, with much singing and fresh creativity resulting in new songs, hymns, and choruses.

All true moves of the Spirit result in moral and ethical reforms, and most have deeply affected the life and history of the nation in which they arose.

Thus the early 1960s saw the beginning of yet another return to the New Testament predominance of the Spirit, with that paramount importance which Jesus Himself gave to the Spirit. In the mid-sixties, almost simultaneously, the Jesus Movement arose among the young, the so-called Neo-Pentecostal movement appeared in the mainline Protestant churches, and there was the beginning of the Catholic Pentecostal movement at Pittsburgh's Duquesne University with four or five laymen. All these groups saw the Person of Jesus as mediated by the Spirit as the only Source of maturity and the deeper life; the only One who can enable us to cope with sin and the evil of these times we are living in; the One who guides, who heals, who empowers.

Within ten years some 400,000 members (a conservative estimate) of mainline Protestant churches in the United States were actively involved in this movement of the Spirit. By the end of the sixties the Catholic Charismatics formed the third—300,000 strong—major group of Pentecostal believers.

But so fast is this renewal now spreading that by the time of the worldwide 1977 Conference on Charismatic Renewal in Kansas City, Missouri (July 20–24), a surprising 50,000 Christians from more than a dozen denominations gathered there. The Catholics were out ahead with 25,000 delegates. There were 6,200 Protestants of mainline denominations; 17,000 non-denominational Christians; 2,000 Pentecostals; 400 Messianic Jews.

How can we explain a phenomenon like this now-worldwide burgeoning of interest in the Helper? How, except to see it as a sovereign move of God to help us all cope once again with the rising tide of evil on our worsening planet Earth!

So many centuries ago, the prophet Ezekiel clearly foretold the two steps that must always take place before any one of us can have the ability to cope with the evil in our world and to possess power for service. . . .

The first step is a readying and cleansing process. "A new spirit will I [God] put within you." That is, God will, through the Spirit, renew and refresh our attitudes, convict us of sin, begin to teach us about obedience, change the thrust and climate of our inner beings. Thus He will be readying us for the crown and glory of His plan—that we, even in our flawed personhood, become the human temples of the Spirit. It was this cleansing and readying that the disciples had been experiencing during Jesus' earthly ministry and during the forty days and then the ten days they were waiting in Jerusalem prior to Pentecost.

But many Christians, because they have never been told that there is something more than regeneration and this "new spirit" within them, stop there. Among these are fine Bible students and church men and women active in the organizational work of their parish. Yet the excitement of the present-day, miracle-working Lord is missing because

their eyes are still on what happened historically, back
during Jesus' earthly ministry and in the early days of the
Church. They have no concept of a living contemporary
Lord living *inside* them, the believers, and working through
them to redeem and heal others.

The second necessary step was clearly foretold by
Ezekiel, "And I will put my Spirit *within* you." It is this
further glorious experience that so many Christians are
discovering freshly in our time.

Still the question comes, can we not receive all of this,
both steps, at the time of our entering-in or being
"born again"? Yes, we could, if we had the knowledge of
what is available, along with the faith and capacity to receive all that. Certainly, there is no limit on God's side; He
is always ready to give and give and give. On the day of
Pentecost, three thousand people *were* able to receive both
a new spirit and the Spirit on the same day.[3]

But most of us are not that open. In actual fact, we
usually do experience being born again and then receiving
the Spirit in two steps as Jesus' own apostles did, as the
Samaritans did,[4] as the disciples at Ephesus did,[5] as did
those present in Cornelius's house to whom Peter spoke,[6]
and as many, many others have down the centuries since.

How important it is to know about this further joyful
gift awaiting us and never to rest until we too have experienced our own personal Pentecost!

HELPFUL READING: John 7:33–39

HIS WORD FOR YOU: The final power of God.
> *Fear not, for I am with you. . . . Yes, from the time of
> the first existence of day and from this day forth I am
> He, and there is no one who can deliver out of My hand.
> I will work and who can hinder or reverse it?*
> (Isaiah 43:13, AMPLIFIED)

PRAYER: *Lord, I see now that my feeling altogether unworthy to be one of Your temples on earth is no excuse
at all. For there is nothing I could ever do that would make
me worthy to receive so great a gift. Any cleansing or prep-
aration necessary must also be Your work in me.*

*I do now, Lord, ask You to flood me on the inside with
that new fresh spirit that can bid You welcome. Help me to*

put no stumbling block in the way of this inner house-keeping and refurbishing and refreshing.

So ready me now to receive the most honored Guest in the cosmos—the Lord of glory. How I praise You that I am living in an era when such a stupendous miracle is possible! Amen.

Part Two

How Do I Receive the Helper?

1 *Hungering and Thirsting for Something More*

If you then, who are evil, know how to give good gifts to your children, how much more will the heavenly Father give the Holy Spirit to those who ask him.

(Luke 11:13, RSV)

Jesus delighted in comparing earthly fathers to His heavenly Father, and then in adding, "But how much more God!" The riches of heaven and of earth all belong to our Father, and He loves to shower them upon us. In Jesus' eyes though, the most precious of all possible gifts is this one of the Holy Spirit.

The first condition then, for receiving this gift so highly esteemed in Jesus' eyes, is our realization of the incomparable value of what we are requesting. For heaven's treasures are not given lightly. Nor will the Father tolerate tepid hearts[1] or honor halfhearted prayer requests.[2] *Lk 18: 1-8*

According to God's Word, without the Holy Spirit we do *Judge & (Widow)* not have: *Rev. 3: 15, 16 – Lukewarm*

Personal awareness of God's love.	Any of the fruits of the Spirit, those lovable characteristics of the Spirit-filled life.
Conviction of who Christ is.	
A message of real help to others.	Real joy.
	Renewal.
The right words to speak in times of stress.	Guidance from God.

43

Comprehension of the thoughts and mind of God.	Healing (except what "nature" or doctors can give us).
Any help in our weakness.	The ability to like or to set our minds on things of the Spirit.
Freedom from slavery to sin and harmful habits.	An Intercessor with the Father.
Any of the gifts of the Spirit.	The Pledge of eternal life.

How then, without the Spirit, can we live anything but a half-life? Are we content to live at a spiritual subsistence level, ineffective and joyless? Realizing this truth can take us from lukewarmness to that hungering and thirsting that Jesus promises us will *always* be satisfied.[3] Mt. 5:6

Early in His ministry, Jesus had stressed the fact that it is only to the thirsty that He will give His living water:

"If any one thirst, let him come to me and drink. He who believes in me, as the scripture has said, 'Out of his heart shall flow rivers of living water.' " Now this he said about the Spirit, which those who believed in him were to receive; for as yet the Spirit had not been given, because Jesus was not yet glorified.[4] Jn 7:37-39

Thus our thirsting and hungering for the Spirit is a necessary condition before we can be granted this gift.

So the world-famous preacher Dr. R. A. Torrey found it just prior to his baptism with the Spirit . . .

I had been a minister for some years before I came to the place where I saw that I had no right to preach until I was definitely baptized with the Holy Ghost. I went to a business friend of mine and said to him in private, "I am never going to enter my pulpit again until I have been baptized with the Holy Spirit and know it, or until God in some way tells me to go."

Then I shut myself up in my study. . . .

But Sunday did not come before the blessing came. . . . I recall the exact spot where I was kneeling in prayer in my study. . . . 1348 North Adams Street,

Minneapolis. If I had understood the Bible as I do now, there need not have passed any days. . . .[5]

Torrey's hungering and thirsting resulted in his asking for the gift of the Spirit with passionate persistence. That is the kind of asking with importunity that Jesus promised us would always be honored.

What then, is the next step in receiving this great gift? Simply that we ask our Lord for the Holy Spirit. Jesus' promise to give the Spirit "to those who ask him" is set in a passage (Today's Reading, below) that stresses importunity and persistence. He tells us to

> . . . Ask and keep on asking, *and it shall be given you;* seek and keep on seeking *and you shall find;* knock and keep on knocking, *and the door shall be opened to you.*[6] *LK. 11:9*

The Greek present imperative verbs "asking," . . . "seeking," . . . "knocking," denote a command, as well as continuing action. The asking required here is no timid tap on the door, but more like a rapping with the passion that results in bloody knuckles.

So dare to ask, first of all, for that gift of hungering and thirsting. Then when out of keen desire, you ask for the gift of the Spirit, you *will* receive Him because Jesus always answers the heart's sincere desire when that desire is in accordance with God's will.

HELPFUL READING: Luke 11:1–13

HIS WORD FOR YOU: How to get our prayers answered.
Now the confidence we have in him is this, that he listens to us whenever we ask anything in accordance with his will; and if we know he listens to whatever we ask, we know we obtain the requests we have made to him.
(I John 5:14, 15, MOFFATT)

PRAYER: *Lord, I do not want to waste the years left to me on this earth. Nor do I want to go through life as a spiritual beggar, in rags, subsisting on the leftovers and the crumbs when I can be a child of the King, dressed in princely garments, feasting at Your banqueting table.*

Thank You, Lord, for making it so clear that rags and crumbs are not Your will; that Your giving, loving heart wants to dress me in the best robe, put a ring on my finger, and welcome me at Your table.

Yet Lord, I know that the gift of the Spirit is not for my joy alone; rather He is given as power for service. You alone can kindle in my heart the deep, fervent desire to be used like that. Take from me lukewarmness. Give me Your own holy passion. Thank You, Lord. Amen.

2 *Accepting Jesus as the Christ*

Therefore it is said, When He [Christ] ascended on high, He led captivity captive—He led a train of vanquished foes—and He bestowed gifts on men.

(Ephesians 4:8, AMPLIFIED)

We live in a time when our world is awash in prophets, gurus, and self-appointed messiahs with immense followings and wealth. Is Jesus then just one more prophet? Many stripes above the rest, to be sure, but still one of many? Each of us has to settle to the satisfaction of his own heart and mind the crucial question of who Jesus is.

Lest we dismiss this too readily, we also need to ponder our disinclination to accept Jesus' claim of exclusiveness in the sense of shutting out all others. Scripture's word on this is worth looking up. Statements like:

No one comes to the Father, but by me.[1] *Jn 14.6*

and:

There is salvation in no one else, for there is no other name under heaven given among men by which we must be saved.[2] *Acts 4.12*

Such statements give us pause today, for in our world they are considered dogmatic, not intellectually or socially acceptable. Some also feel that they are not even nationally permissible because they go against our present interpretation of our Constitutional guarantee of "freedom of religion."

Thus each of us has an important decision to make here. Is Jesus really who He claimed to be—the *only* begotten Son of the Father, "very God of very God?" Is He entitled to be called "the Christ?" For the name *Christ* means "the Messiah," the One prophesied through all the centuries. After all, even men are sometimes called "lord," but there can be only one Christus—the Crowned One.

Until we catch a glimpse of the full glory of this crowned Christ, of the honors heaped upon Him, of the extent of the power the Father has placed in His hands, we can never grasp the significance of Jesus' question, "Who do you say that I am?"

For the Christ is the King of Kings, and the Lord of Lords.[3] Rev 19:16

The Apostle John heaps up words to tell us that upon Jesus' return to heaven, He received power, and riches, and wisdom, and strength, and honor, and glory, and blessing.[4] Rev 5:12

Not only our small planet Earth, but all of the cosmos has been put under His authority, subject to His word alone. This includes everything in the heavens, our earth and all of the planetary system, as well as the world below —that domain of evil spirits in rebellion against God's authority.[5] Col 2:10, Eph 3:10; 4:8-10; I Cor. 15:24

But we miss the point of Christ's crowning until we see His coronation as another step in God's plan to lift us human beings out of the plight we have been in since the Fall. It staggers us to think that we, you and I, and our planet Earth are still today the passion of Christ's heart.

What happened at Pentecost is that the Holy Spirit was sent as Christ's coronation gift to us. Through the Helper, all of the crowned Christ's resources and riches and graces and wisdom and power became available to us humans in order that we might "reign as kings in life."[6] Could any plan have been more wonderful? Ro. 6:17

Jesus dramatized all of this for us in His incomparable parable of the prodigal Son.[7] What delighted the father's heart, pleased him most? Not the elder brother staying dutifully at home, toiling incessantly for the father. . . . "These many years do I serve thee, and yet—"

And yet the elder boy's heart had found no rest. He

Lk 15:11-32

knew no joy in all |
any progress in his
full of grievances, gr
tive and unable to re
did not please his fath

What delighted the
was willing to let his fa

Amazingly, not a wo
father speak when his w
Instead, there was total
and all-out rejoicing tha
receive of the father's bo
should make merry, and b

This is the gospel. This ....gcss of the
Father's heart, reflected i ... . way by the crowned
Christ.

Are we then ready to accept Jesus as this crowned One,
the reigning Christ of John's Book of Revelation, the all-
powerful, miracle-working Lord of the universe?

This was the question my friend Madame Bilquis Sheikh
struggled with one day ten years ago in her palatial country
home in Pakistan.[9] Born of a wealthy family influential in
government circles, she had been reared a devoted Muslim.
Having been introduced to Christianity through a direct
sovereign move of God, Madame Sheikh had reached out
to talk to a missionary couple and to one nun. But she was
still confused. How could she finally know which was truth
—the Koran—or the Bible? And which was really the
Anointed of God: Mohammed—or Jesus Christ?

She remembered that the nun had suggested, "Try talking to God as if He were your Father." But what Muslim
could even think of talking to Allah like a father?

The next day, December 12th, was Madame Sheikh's
birthday. She awoke thinking of her parents and of the
extraordinarily happy birthday celebrations all through her
childhood. Her father had never been too busy to receive
his little "Keecha" in his study, to set aside whatever he
was doing to help in any way he could.

Savoring these remembrances, her heart filled with gratitude, Madame Sheikh murmured a thanksgiving to her
earthly father, "Oh thank you for being like that, father."

Then a shaft of understanding hit her. If her earthly
father could be like that, then her heavenly Father—

...t, she sank to her knees by the ... in her life shyly called God "My

...loose in her. He was there! Like a hand ... head. She could sense His presence, His

...Madame Sheikh rose from her knees three hours ...ny tears later, she had her answer—resoundingly. ...e on the table where she had left them, lay the Koran ...d the Bible side by side. Now she knew which was true —the Book that had led her to her Father and to that other One whose glory He will share with no other prophet— Jesus, the Christ.

HELPFUL READING: John 6:51, 54; 8:12, 28; 10:1–9, 33, 36; 14:6

HIS WORD FOR YOU: The permanence of work done in the Lord.

I know that, whatsoever God doeth, it shall be for ever: nothing can be put to it, nor any thing taken from it. . . .
(Ecclesiastes 3:14, KJV)

PRAYER: *Lord, I know that You were fearlessly dogmatic because You were simply speaking truth, telling it as it is. Just as two added to two must equal four, and no necessity for tolerance or broadmindedness can change that, even so there is no way to change the only route by which we humans can find our way to God.*

In a world where fuzziness and equivocation reign, I thank You for Your clarity and insistence on truth.

And Lord, my heart can't contain my gratitude that You are even now running down the road to meet me. Me— also a prodigal who has failed You so often. That You would dress me in princely raiment and prepare a banquet for me! This staggers me, Lord, and makes me very humble, and my love for You pours out in return.

Open my eyes now to the riches and fullness of Your magnificent plan. And Lord, this really is a daring prayer . . . I ask You to make me, like that other prodigal, a good receiver of all Your bounty. Amen.

3 Deciding to Obey the Good Shepherd

The Holy Spirit whom God has given to those who obey him.

(Acts 5:32, RSV)

The Lord gives the Holy Spirit to those who obey Him. This in no way contradicts the fact that God's gifts can be received only by grace (the unmerited favor of God) through faith, because faith (trusting God) and obedience are but two sides of the same thing.

Nor can trust ever end in just intellectual faith or lip service to faith. When it is the real thing, it will spill over into action—and that will mean obedience.[1] James 2:17-22

For how can the Good Shepherd lead His sheep to green pastures and protect them from harm if the sheep refuse to follow the Shepherd? Our world today is such that the difficulties and evils each human being must walk through in his lifetime on earth are something like threading one's way across heavily mined terrain. Desperately, we need the all-knowledge and the all-power of the Good Shepherd. Yet there is no way He can help and protect us in the tender and minute way He longs to unless we trust His love enough to obey.

Kay Peters, wife of Dr. John Peters, the founder of that great organization World Neighbors, tells in an upcoming book of a night when she learned the hard way the importance of minute, unquestioning obedience to the Spirit's leading. After rigorous months of work on his doctorate at

51

Yale, John was teaching college classes with "moonlighting" teaching on the side for much needed income. A degree of exhaustion had set in.

In the middle of an exceptionally cold winter's night, Kay awoke to hear her husband getting out of bed. The inner voice of the Spirit spoke a clear, strong warning to her, "Go with John."

But as most of us would, Kay allowed her mind to get in the way. "Why, I never go to the bathroom with John. Why should I go now?"

So instead of obeying, she asked, "John, what's the matter?"

"I think I'm catching a cold," was the reply. "Just going to see if I can find some medicine."

Reassured, Kay quenched the warning voice inside her and snuggled more deeply into the covers.

Suddenly, from the bathroom came the sound of a terrifying crash. Leaping out of bed and dashing for the bathroom, Kay was aghast at what she saw. John had fainted and fallen in the tub. In the process the ceramic tile soap dish had been torn from the wall. The broken pieces had deeply gashed the side of his face and torn loose the lower part of his right ear.

Her husband was unconscious. Like a broken doll, his long body was draped incongruously over the side of the tub. His face rested on the bottom with a wide stream of blood already pulsing down the drain.

Although it turned out that Dr. Peters had had a concussion and did lose a great deal of blood, this emergency was in the end beautifully handled by the healing work of the Spirit. For God, unlike us, holds no grudges when we fail to obey. His only desire is to *help us*.

Long after the crisis was past and the Peterses were praising God for the way it had turned out, Kay was still pondering:

When was I going to start obeying consistently? If I had done so before the accident occurred, the whole tragic episode could have been avoided. I had to sing my song of rejoicing in a minor key.

When Jesus promised the Holy Spirit, He stressed (at least three times) that this gift was for the obedient. Here are some statements to look up and ponder: John 14:15, 16, 21, 23; Acts 5:32.

Often we stumble because we sense that we are like the apostles before Pentecost: they wanted to obey, but had not the ability to do so. There is then the temptation to reason, "Even though I mean to obey Jesus now and tell Him so, how do I know that I'll be able to obey Him in the future? I don't trust myself. So how can I ever meet this condition of obedience in connection with asking for the Spirit?"

Even on this seemingly impossible level, there is good news. When we obey the light we have now, set the rudder of our will to heed and follow the loving help the Spirit wants to give us in the future, and tell Jesus so, we find that He counts our willingness and purpose as obedience. From then on, the glad tidings are that the Spirit Himself will increasingly supply us with the *ability* to obey. God is ahead of us here, as always. He knows both our mistrust of ourselves and our weakness in obedience, so the glad promise is that we shall be able to obey, only

> [Not in your own strength] for it is God Who is all the while effectually at work in you—energizing and creating in you the power and desire—both to will and to work for His good pleasure and satisfaction and delight.[2] *Phil. 2:13*

Let us then not allow any discouragement about ourselves to halt our determination for the Spirit's full presence and help in our life. How can we *not* want to obey when we begin to comprehend the magnitude of the Helper's love and complete goodwill for us!

HELPFUL READING: Acts 9:10–19

HIS WORD FOR YOU: My heart, His home.
   The (Holy) Spirit [Himself]—indwelling your innermost being and personality.
   May Christ through your faith [actually] dwell—settle down, abide, make His permanent home—in your hearts! May you be rooted deep in love and founded securely on love....

   (Ephesians 3:16, 17, AMPLIFIED)

PRAYER: *"Take, O Lord, and receive my entire liberty, my memory, my understanding, and my whole will. All that I am, all that I have, Thou hast given me, and I will give it back again to Thee." Amen.*
                    (Saint Ignatius Loyola)

4 Inviting Jesus as the Baptizer

He . . . Upon Whom you shall see the Spirit descend and remain, that One is He Who baptizes with the Holy Spirit.

The Comforter . . . Whom I [Jesus] will send to you. . . .
(John 1:33; 15:26, AMPLIFIED)

Scripture makes it clear that Jesus Himself is the only One who can baptize us with the Spirit. That is why there must always be the first step of commitment to Jesus (being "born again") before we can receive the fullness of His Spirit.

These facts shed light on a little vignette in John's Gospel. In one of Jesus' first post-resurrection appearances, He appeared and spoke to His apostles who had gathered behind locked doors for fear of the Jews.

Peace to you! [Just] as the Father has sent Me forth, so I am sending you.

And having said this, He breathed on [them] and said to them, Receive (admit) the Holy Spirit![1]

The incident has been a puzzling one since we know that the fullness of the Spirit could not be given until Pentecost. By "breathing upon them" was not Jesus dramatizing for His apostles the fact that the Spirit could be imparted only by *His* breath, His very life?

55

He knew that when the day of Pentecost finally came, the apostles would recall this scene and would then understand that always the Spirit must be connected with His own Person.

We twentieth-century Christians can receive the Spirit no other way, except by Jesus, the Baptizer . . .

In 1963 the Episcopal rector Graham Pulkingham was sent to the Church of the Redeemer in the East End of Houston, Texas. It was a poverty-stricken slum area with a racial mixture of blacks, Mexican-Americans, and poor whites. Six churches of different denominations in this area had already given up and moved away.

It looked as if the Church of the Redeemer was about to meet the same fate. Within seven months of Graham's arrival, the parish had lost seventy-five families and a third of its revenue. The vestry voted to close the church except for one Sunday morning service.

But the gigantic needs of the East End community lay heavily on the young rector's heart. The sheep were starving and astray. Who was going to feed them? And *how?*

Then Graham heard of David Wilkerson's work in the slums of Brooklyn. There the situation was even worse than in Houston's East End. Yet there the sheep were being fed. Miracles were happening with the narcotics pushers, the prostitutes, and the teenagers who were mainlining drugs.

In mid-August of that year the way was opened for Graham to spend four days with David Wilkerson. For the first three days, he saw all the different facets of David's work in the Brooklyn slums. The afternoon of the fourth day found Graham in the book-lined library of an old house with Dave and two other men. Out of the blue, Dave turned and said to Graham, "I bear witness about you—kneel down, I want to pray." The young rector knelt and the three men laid their hands on his head.

Let Graham tell what happened then . . .

Soon . . . all awareness of the men and their prayers, of the room, and even of myself was obliterated by the immense presence of God's power. . . . The very foundations of my soul shook violently. . . . *Those prayers for a powerful ministry are being answered! Right now! Great God, can it be?*

In a moment of breathless adoration, all my longing for love was satisfied and my inner being was swept clean of defilement. . . . I bowed my head to the ground and still kneeling, wept convulsively.

"We can go now, the Baptizer's here," said Dave Wilkerson to his companions, and they departed.

Sometime later I rose to my feet with a strange buoyancy. The Baptizer had done His work, and I knew that from then on my ministry would be of Godly power.[2]

So it turned out. In the years that followed, the Church of the Redeemer reopened its doors and its heart to the East End folk. What has happened is a thrilling story. I have been there and have seen this former slum area transformed now into a Christian community so vital that it is making news all around the world.

Jesus' own bestowal of the gift of the Holy Spirit made all the difference!

HELPFUL READING: John 7:34–39

HIS WORD FOR YOU: How beautiful He is!
How beautiful upon the mountains are the feet of him who brings good tidings, who publishes peace . . . who says to Zion, Your God reigns!
(Isaiah 52:7, AMPLIFIED)

PRAYER: *Lord Jesus, I thank You that all of the Father's good gifts are now Yours to bestow on us, Your children, including the greatest gift of all, the Spirit Himself.*
I begin to see that without the Spirit my personal life and my church's life are as inert and dead as lifeless clay. Show me now anything in me that would hinder or block my receiving this new life. Cleanse my heart, Lord, and prepare it to be a fit dwelling place for You. In joyous anticipation. Amen.

5 *Being Willing to Be Put to Work*

But whosoever will be great among you, shall be your minister:

And whosoever of you will be the chiefest, shall be servant of all.

For even the Son of man came not to be ministered unto, but to minister. . . .

(Mark 10:43–45, KJV)

Jesus' resurrection appearances included long talks with His disciples and some explicit orders: they were to "tarry in Jerusalem" until the descent of the Helper into their lives. The purpose of this tarrying? So that they would have the Helper's wisdom, guidance, and power to become His witnesses, beginning in Jerusalem, then in ever-widening circles.[1] Acts 1.8

Note that Jesus did *not* tell them or us that the gift of the Helper is for our own spiritual development or perfection. Nor is it even for getting rid of our selfishness by dying to self. Nor for our happiness or joy or euphoria in new freer-form fellowship. Not even so that we can get our prayer needs met.

All of those results will follow as dividends, provided we accept Jesus' top priority—witnessing to the world out there (now under Satan's dominion) in loving service. Indeed, so long as we seek the baptism of the Spirit with ourselves primarily in mind—for *our* Spiritual growth, for *our* peace of mind and joy, for *our* prayers answered—then the Helper always withholds a measure of himself.

58

The Holy Spirit will not come to us in His fullness until we see and assent to His priority—His passion for ministry. Are we ready to give ourselves to others? He will accept no excuses about our inadequacy in this way or that. Giving us adequacy is *His* business. That's what His coming to us is all about. So—are we ready to be His "living sacrifice" to carry His love to His needy children—anytime, anywhere?

The Helper has used a failure of mine in this regard to teach me how much He means business about service. One night about two years ago I was alone in our home, so had carefully locked all doors. Close to midnight, I was ready for bed and about to turn out the lights.

Suddenly, there came a loud knocking on the front door. Asking who it was through the still-closed door, I heard the voice of an acquaintance whose sister was dying of cancer in a nearby town.

As the midnight visitor and I then talked face to face, I learned that she had come to ask me to drive with her then, that night, to pray at her sister's bedside. There were some complications, including the fact that she had not telephoned the sick woman's husband to tell him of this nocturnal visit. So I demurred, asking if I could go to the bedside the following day. Reluctantly, my visitor agreed and left.

But the following morning the sick woman was moved to the hospital. That day when I got to her room, I found that she had sunk into deep coma. No one was around—no member of the family, no hospital personnel. Quietly I sat there and prayed for her, but there was a sinking feeling of anticlimax. She died later that day.

Questions kept pounding at me. . . . What would have happened had I gone on that night? Only God knows. But at least the sick woman would have been conscious. Was there an important word the Helper wanted her to hear?

So the Spirit has used this incident to teach me. With incisiveness, He has put His finger where it hurts: "Not enough flexibility or promptness in obeying Me. So you drive to another town in the middle of the night. Forget sleep. Forget your convenience. Even ignore certain amenities, as you see them. When I say 'Go,' I'll take care of the amenities too."

In searching out the Helper's dealings with some towering Christian figures around the turn of the century—

Dwight L. Moody, R. A. Torrey, C. I. Scofield, J. Wilbur Chapman, A. B. Simpson, Billy Sunday—I find that they were given an emphasis on the "gift of the Holy Spirit for service" or what they called "soul-winning service." This relates directly back to Jesus' orders to be His witnesses all over the world.[1]

Moody's statement is representative of this group:

> In some sense, and to some extent, the Holy Spirit dwells in every believer, but there is another gift which may be called the gift of the Holy Spirit for service. This gift, it strikes me, is entirely distinct and separate from conversion and assurance. God has a great many children who have no power, and the reason is, they have not the gift of the Holy Ghost for service. . . . They have not sought this gift.[2]

How sad if the modern movement of the Spirit is better known for chorus-singing, hand-clapping, lifted hands, and great mass meetings than for service.

Since the Helper is Jesus' own presence among us, we can be certain that in our time, as always, He will still be girded with a towel, washing our feet, lovingly ministering.

And we—are we better than our Master?

The fullness and overflow of the Spirit will come to us only as we too say "Yes" to Him, reach for the towel and the basin of water, and get to work.

HELPFUL READING: John 13:3–17; 21:11–17

HIS WORD FOR YOU: To those in need of rescuing.
Strengthen the weak hands, and make firm the feeble and tottering knees.

Say to those that are of a fearful and hasty heart, Be strong, fear not! Behold, your God will come with vengeance, with the recompense of God; He will come and save you.

(Isaiah 35:3, 4, AMPLIFIED)

PRAYER: *O Lord Jesus, I can see that my adventures with You haven't even begun until I am willing to go to work for You. All my excuses and rationalizations of inadequacy are no good: that's really saying that You are in-*

adequate to work through me as You please, once I am willing.

So Lord, here I am. I know that it's a hazardous prayer because You will rush to answer it—but take me, use me.

I see it now! Even as You bring those staggering needs to me and to those with whom I am in close fellowship, that's when You will give us faith-strengthening demonstrations of Your present-day power.

As You plunge us in over our heads, that's when we will be given the particular gifts of the Spirit we need.

Lord, Your ways are incredible. You are incredible—and I love You. How great You are! Lord, I worship You. Amen.

6 Repentance and Baptism: Rising to New Life

When they heard this they were cut to the heart, and said to Peter and the apostles, "Friends, what are we to do?"

"Repent," said Peter, "repent and be baptized, every one of you, in the name of Jesus the Messiah for the forgiveness of your sins; and you will receive the gift of the Holy Spirit."

(Acts 2:37, 38, NEB)

Acts 2:14-39

As in imagination we listen to Peter preaching this, his first sermon[1] after the startling events of Pentecost, we can scarcely believe what we are hearing. This confident, articulate, impassioned, fearless man is *Peter?* The same big rough fisherman who habitually said and did the wrong thing and was so cowardly that at his Master's crisis-moment he crumbled even under a few questions from a servant girl!

But this is a new Peter. The old timid, ineffective man is now submerged in and filled with the Holy Spirit. And with startling results! Every word of this first sermon goes to its target and so convinces and convicts his listeners that on the spot three thousand of them become followers of Jesus.

In our time we need to know what exactly Peter meant by preaching the necessity "to repent." We are told that the word means "to turn around" or "to change one's mind." But to change our minds about what? About our appraisal of the old life we have been living so far.

Peter was a case in point, and we can see ourselves reflected in him. In the old days he had had plenty of drive, abundant energy and determination, some obvious talents, even good motivation—he meant well. Yes, and the burly, gruff fisherman deeply loved his Master and wanted to please Him.

Yet none of that was good enough. So this new Peter had repented of his old life and his effort to handle it on his own. That is, his appraisal of that old self before Pentecost had long since been a crisp "no good." After all, Peter and the other one hundred nineteen gathered in the Upper Room were asking the *Holy* Spirit to come and live in them, and holiness and cleanliness cannot live in a sin-ridden slum.

Rees Howells, Welsh coal miner (1879–1950) whom God mightily used in the ministry of prayer-intercession, has written of the first time he met the Spirit. It was as real an experience as Rees' meeting with the Savior had been three years before . . .

He said to me, "As the Savior had a body, so I dwell in the cleansed temple of the believer. I am God and I am come to ask you to give your body to Me that I may work through it. . . ."

He made it very plain that He would never share my life . . . but there were many things dear to me and I knew I couldn't keep one of them. . . .

He put His finger on each part of my self-life, and I had to decide in cold blood. He could never take a thing away until I gave my consent. . . . He was not going to take any superficial surrender. . . .[2]

So real was this repentance period for Rees that the process took five days and many tears, during which he lost seven pounds.

The Spirit may point out to any of us a wide gamut of sins—any unforgiveness or resentment harbored in the heart—no matter how seemingly justified; estrangements; any still-hidden dishonesty or unfaithfulness; indulgences; our particular use of self-will; and certainly, any involvement with the occult, however innocent or far back. This would include fortune-telling, spiritualism, horoscopes, playing with Ouija boards, drugs that opened the unconscious to spirit powers, and any involvement with cults directed by any power other than Jesus Christ. Any such uncovered sin needs to be confessed, followed by our acceptance of God's forgiveness, and a renouncing of Satan and all his works.

Sometimes the Spirit will then go to the other end of the spectrum and point out something seemingly trivial saying, "That also must go." This can be puzzling. Would God concern Himself with a seeming triviality? The experience of other Christians down the ages can help us here. Their writings tell us that there is no such thing as a small or trivial sin because all sin is an act of self in rebellion against God. And the Spirit knows that repentance becomes real to us only as He makes it very specific.

Yet because the Helper is always a realist and insists on being thoroughgoing, He is after much more than throwing out some sin-debris here and there.

Again, Rees Howells' experience illustrates this. After the Spirit had pointed out to Rees those things to be jettisoned, then . . .

Like Isaiah, I saw the holiness of God, and seeing Him, I saw my own corrupt nature. It wasn't sin I saw, but my nature, self . . . that thing which came from the Fall. . . .[8]

So how can we deal with something as basic as the sin-nature with which we were born?

Usually, we try to rid ourselves of selfishness or irritability and a temper that erupts, or whatever, by confessing and repenting of our sin, setting our will against it, and working at getting rid of our bad habit—with God's help, of course.

But that is not Scripture's prescription for our deliverance. The problem is that this is our fallen nature acting, and that nature—no matter how patched-up, improved, or disciplined—can have no part in God's kingdom.[4]

In this impasse, Scripture has glad news for us:

We know that our old (unrenewed) self was nailed to the cross with Him [Jesus]. . . .[5]

and

> Are you ignorant of the fact that all of us who have
> been baptized into Christ Jesus were baptized into His
> death?[6] *Ro. 6.3*

With the Cross, God wiped out the old creation that was
flawed in Eden. The gospel's momentous news is not only
that Jesus died on that Cross, but that you and I and our
flawed natures also died with Him.

Here is a homely illustration of this. . . . If I place a
dollar bill between the pages of a book, then burn the
book, the dollar bill goes up in flames along with the book.
Just as surely, each of us humans, together with all the sins
we would commit in our lifetime, along with our capacity
for sin—the sin principle in us—died on that Cross.

How can I be certain of this? Because God says so. This
great truth is all over the New Testament. In addition to
the passages above, here are some further statements with
which to satisfy your own mind and heart: Galatians 2:20,
Colossians 3:3, II Timothy 2:11. *Eph 2:5, 6*

Not only that, even as I was "in" Christ on His Cross, so
I also rose with Him,[7] have been set in the heavenlies with
Him, and I am now complete only in Him.[8] *Col 2:10*

So this means that God will not allow us (being dead—
defunct) any Christian experience in our old fleshly nature,
nothing apart from Jesus. God is not going to drop into
our laps, as a package commodity, unselfishness or a loving
disposition or any virtue.

Instead, He has promised me Jesus' resurrection life in
me. Thus it will be Jesus' selflessness and patience and love
manifested in my life—not my own.

So now as I let go my old tired efforts at self-improvement
and step out to trust Jesus' fresh, exhilarating resurrected
life in me, to my amazement, I find solid ground beneath
my feet.

Perhaps you have wondered about the meaning of those
adult Believer's-Baptisms in backyard swimming pools or
at the edge of the ocean. Many of those participating are
Christians who were christened as babies. Now that the
Helper has revealed to them what being baptized into Jesus'
death really means, they long to experience leaving their
old self under water with the joy of rising to a new life in
the Spirit.

Who but a loving heavenly Father could have thought of that!

HELPFUL READING: Acts 8:25–40

HIS WORD FOR YOU: He never condemns us.
Therefore, [there is] now no condemnation for those who are in Christ Jesus.
(Romans 8:1, RSV)

PRAYER: *Lord Jesus, I do need a housecleaning on the inside. It takes courage for me to ask this: bring to my remembrance anything I need to confess to You. I want to get rid of all the debris. Especially my resentment against _____, and my stubborn unwillingness to love _____. I give all this negativity to You. You take it, Lord.*

And how grateful I am that I don't need to be encumbered with my sin-nature, that it too was nailed to Your Cross. But Lord, this is not yet real to me. I ask the Helper to grant me a personal revelation of this great truth to bring it alive for me.

Show me now how to claim my new life in You, Lord Jesus, and to walk hour by hour in that fresh new dimension. And thank You for the feeling of adventure! Amen.

7 Accepting God's Grace

The wind blows . . . where it will; and though you hear its sound, yet you neither know where it comes from nor where it goes. So it is with every one who is born of the Spirit.

(John 3:8, AMPLIFIED)

We have seen that there are definite steps to be taken if we are to receive the baptism of the Spirit. There must be a real thirst resulting in specifically asking Jesus Himself for this gift. There must be repentance, forgiveness, and a break with one's old life. There must be the set of the will to obedience, and the desire and intention to use one's life (no matter what one's vocation or profession) for ministry to others.

To these must be added one more condition—the fact that there is no way we can receive the Spirit except by a present-tense faith. For nothing any of us could ever do or stop doing can earn this or any of heaven's gifts. Forever and forever they are given only by grace—which is the unmerited favor of a loving Father.[1] *Gal. 3:1-5*

Yet once we realize how unworthy we are to ask the Helper to come and live inside us, then on what basis can we find the faith to ask for and receive this gift of gifts? It is a relief to realize that the basis for faith here has nothing to do with us and everything to do with the Lord Jesus. Scripture makes it plain that the coming of the Spirit at Pentecost (and ever since) is the result of Jesus' exaltation, glorification, and crowning in heaven.[2] *Acts 2:32,33*

Watchman Nee, preeminent Bible expositor, expresses it succinctly: "The Holy Spirit has not been poured out on

67

you or me to prove how great we are, but to prove the greatness of the Son of God."[3]

In other words, the outpouring of the Spirit is earth's evidence and proof of what happened after Jesus' ascension: not only of the magnificence of His crowning in heaven, but of His very real coronation power. Paul strains for words in trying to describe this:

> When he raised him [Jesus] from the dead and made him sit at his right hand in the heavenly places, far above all rule and authority and power and dominion, and above every name that is named. . . .[4] *Eph 1:20, 21*

Then since Christ's power, meant to be mediated through the Spirit, is our triumphant Lord's gift to us, how tragic if any of us fail to appropriate it!

Once I had realized all of this after I had spent the summer of 1944 studying the Scripture about it, I knew how impossible my Christian walk would be without the Helper. I also saw that even in the Acts accounts there was wide diversity in how different individuals received the Spirit. Sometimes He would come through the laying on of hands or after the sacrament of baptism, sometimes not. Some received the gift of tongues at the moment of their Spirit-baptism, others did not. It was obvious that the Spirit cannot be pigeonholed or preguessed or manipulated, and that we had best not try. Jesus gave Nicodemus the perfect analogy: who can preguess or control the wind?

So, since at that time I had no group to lay hands on me, very quietly and undramatically I asked for the gift of the Spirit. The setting was my bedroom with no other human being present. I knew too that when we accept one of heaven's gifts like that—so quietly in the now—we cannot demand instantaneous proof that the Lord has heard and answered. For that would be walking by sight, not faith at all.

Still, being a practical person, I couldn't help wondering how long this blind-faith period would last. What about Jesus' promise made on the eve of His glorification at the dawning of the era of the Helper, that He *will* manifest Himself to us?[5] *Jn 14:21*

That Jesus should have promised to reveal Himself to us in this new era is not surprising. After all, the Helper is a

Person whose work is to point to and reveal Jesus. And, I reminded myself, any person dwelling with us would inevitably reveal himself by his personality traits—his ways, deeds, and words.

As I searched out the experience of other Christians on this (such as Dwight L. Moody, Charles G. Finney, R. A. Torrey, John Wesley, Sammy Morris—the African boy, Evan Roberts, A. B. Simpson, Watchman Nee, and many in our own time), I learned that some had had manifestations of the Helper's presence—such as feelings like a series of electric shocks, waves of liquid love pouring through one's body, feelings of impossible joy, speaking a heavenly language—while others had not.

Scripture makes it clear that the Helper is not fond of spectacular ways of exhibitionism. After all, no trumpets herald the pinky-gray opalescent dawn. No bugles announce the opening of a rosebud. God speaks not in the thunder or the roaring wind, rather in a "still, small voice."

So I knew that although I should not deny their validity, I should guard against demanding a highly emotional or dramatic experience as initial proof of my baptism in the Spirit. Our triumphant Lord does not need to prove anything. If Jesus wanted to grant me some dramatic evidence, fine. But I would wait for *His* timing on any manifestation at all of the Helper's presence.

Nothing overt happened that first day. I experienced no waves of liquid love or ecstatic joy. But then in the next few days, quietly but surely, the heavenly Guest made known His presence in my heart. He began talking to me at odd moments throughout the day. Sometimes even as I would open my mouth to speak, there would be a sharp check on the inside. I soon learned that the Helper sought to prevent careless words or critical words or even too many words. Nor would He tolerate even a trace of sarcasm, or faithless words of doubt or fear.

So day by day came the evidence that after I had asked the Helper to enter and take charge, He had done exactly that.

This evidence mounted. The Helper now sought to guide me even in life's small decisions in order to smooth my way or save me time and futile effort. I also found, as has many another, that the manifestation of His presence on which the Spirit places highest value is the power to witness effectively to others of Jesus.

He then entered into my prayer life and began directing that. He became the major creative Agent in my writing. In the months that followed and indeed, on down the years, He would methodically bring one area of life after another under His control—health, finances, ambition, reputation. I soon realized that the baptism of the Holy Spirit was no one-time experience, rather a process that would continue throughout my lifetime. True, there was that initial infilling. But how well I knew that I had not thereby been elevated to instant sainthood. In my humanness, self kept creeping back in, so I needed repeated fillings if I were ever to become the mature person God meant me to be.

Not only that, I would discover that the special gifts of the Spirit along with the fruit of His presence—His character within us—are also marvelously authentic evidence of His presence.

And the very dramatic manifestations? Some of those were to come later. Some I have never yet experienced. Yet that September would come the crown of all—the presence of the Risen Lord, the literal fulfilling of "and I will love him [her] and manifest myself to him."[6]

HELPFUL READING: John 3:1–21

HIS WORD FOR YOU: Our Father's good will for us.
What father among you, if his son asks for a loaf of bread, will give him a stone; or if he asks for a fish, will . . . give him a serpent . . . ?

If you then, evil-minded as you are, know how to give good gifts . . . to your children, how much more will your heavenly Father give the Holy Spirit to those who ask . . . Him!
(Luke 11:11, 13, AMPLIFIED)

PRAYER: *Lord, I have accepted the challenge of Your great promise. I have asked for the gift of the Helper. I have bidden Him welcome as He enters my heart to take possession. So now, by faith, I accept Your sure promise that this is done, that I have received the Spirit.*

I wait patiently now for these tokens of the Helper's presence that shall reveal that He is not only with me but in me.

Help me too never to fall into the trap of thinking of

*the Helper as a servant to do my bidding; rather create in
me the willingness to be Your servant, Lord, for Your
work to be done through me. Then only will I know the
fullness of the Helper's presence. In Your strong name, I
pray. Amen.*

Part Three

How the Helper Meets My Everyday Needs

1 *He Saves Me Time*

Walk as children of light . . . and try to learn what is pleasing to the Lord.

(Ephesians 5:8, 10, RSV)

Often we think of God as One concerned only with our spirit's welfare, not with the affairs of everyday life—like how we handle the hours of our day. We are inclined to resist the Spirit's inner nudges because we suspect that what God wants "for our own good" would be about as welcome as castor oil.

The truth is quite the opposite. Yet it is only a daily experimental walk with the Spirit that will prove this to us. He is concerned about our spirit's health and growth, but He is also attentive to what is of present, practical importance to us. We will find that it is to our intelligent self-interest to become sensitive to the Helper's loving directions. These come in several forms: urges, promptings, uneasiness . . . stops. We have all known these.

So often I have experienced it. One evening my husband Peter and I had planned to see a particular movie. It turned out to be a disappointing evening in every way. Long queues made it impossible even to get near the theatre. Then a store which we thought we might visit proved to be closed.

On the way home, having been frustrated at every turn, Peter and I compared notes and found that earlier, each of us had had a strong inner feeling that we should not go. But neither had verbalized this, fearing to disappoint the other, especially since there was no reason to give except the inner direction. We learned an important lesson that evening about the Spirit's desire to spare us frustration and wasted time.

The well-known author Agnes Sanford relates a similar type of experience. She had an important engagement in Richmond, Virginia. Several hours previous to departure time, however, Agnes was aware of a strong "stop" from the Spirit. Since her mission was the Lord's work and she could see no reason for such guidance, she disregarded it and started.

Before the train reached Richmond, there was a wreck on the track ahead. The train stopped in time, but the passengers were forced to sit up all night as they waited for the track to be cleared. "Afterward," Agnes said, "I realized that the inner Voice had been trying to warn me of this."

We need the practice of daily experimentation in hearing the Spirit's voice. Since not all inner desires, urgings, or even voices are from God, He has graciously given us a number of ways of testing out such inner directions.

It is important to remember that the inner Voice will never bid us do anything shady, dishonest, impure, unloving, or selfish in the sense that it hurts another. Nor will He ever tell us anything contrary to Scripture because God will not contradict Himself.

Then too, as often as possible this kind of guidance should be checked out with a fellow Christian. Finally, one of the Helper's special gifts is that of the discerning of spirits. He has promised that each church fellowship constituted by Him will have one or more individuals to whom He has given this needed gift for the benefit of all in the fellowship.[1]   ICo. 12. 4—10

However, I found that in the everydayness of life when there was not time for this more thorough checking, and when the inner guidance did not obviously violate any of God's loving laws or hurt another, it was important to obey and thus experiment with it. That was how I learned to recognize the Helper's voice.

Nothing will so strengthen our faith and convince us of the tender love of God and of His concern for even the minutiae of our lives as this daily walk in the Spirit.

HELPFUL READING: Acts 10:17–24; 27:1–3; 9–11

HIS WORD FOR YOU: He will turn troubles into highways.

And I will make all my mountains a way, and my highways shall be raised up.

(Isaiah 49:11, RSV)

PRAYER: *Lord Jesus, so often I ignore or ride roughshod over these strong inner feelings supplied by the Spirit. What is lack of trust in You, Lord, change that. Give me Your own confidence in the Father's never-failing love and goodwill.*

What is willfulness in me, Lord, change that too. For nothing could be more foolish than thinking I know better than You do. Help me this day, no matter how busy I get, to listen and to obey. Amen.

the Holy Spirits loving directions
— of several forms:

    1. urges

    2. promptings

    3. uneasiness

    4. Stops

Remember — That Inner Voice will Never bid us do anything —

shady
dishonest
impure   in the sense
unloving   that it hurts
selfish   others.

★ — never anything Contrary to
Scripture
often check out with Christian friend

2 He Guides My Actions

The Holy Spirit said, "Set apart for me Barnabas and Saul for the work to which I have called them." . . . So, being sent out by the Holy Spirit, they went down to Seleucia.
(Acts 13:2, 4, RSV)

The setting for the Spirit's special message to Barnabas and Saul (Paul) was the first little Christian Church in Antioch. This city was one of the most corrupt in the Roman Empire at a time when corruption, poverty and flagrantly gross sins were rampant.

Paul and Barnabas had been ministering together in the Antioch church for only a year. The work seemed such a tiny, flickering light in the great pagan city. Yet here was the guidance of the Spirit directing the little new church to give up its two top leaders.

The fellowship's human reaction might well have been, "But—but Paul's and Barnabas's work has only begun here. How can we get along without them? Besides, shouldn't young new recruits be the ones to be sent out for their training rather than our most capable leaders?"

Yet that was not the reaction of the Antioch fellowship. Instead, they fasted and prayed, asking the Spirit, "Have we heard You correctly?" Having confirmed that they had, they then laid hands on Barnabas and Paul and sent them out with everyone's blessing.[1] They trusted the Spirit to take care of His own in Antioch and of His still-struggling church there.

From my own experience and that of many others, I know that the Spirit's guidance is just as real in our cen-

78

tury as it was in Paul's day. As a college girl attending
Atlanta's Westminster Presbyterian Church where Peter
Marshall pastored, I first heard him tell the story of this
same kind of guidance in his life . . .

Born in the industrial town of Coatbridge, Scotland, he
felt the call of God on his life at age twenty-one. His "tap
on the shoulder" came one night at the Buchanan Street
Kirk after a call for recruits by the London Missionary
Society.

At the time Peter thought that "the Chief" (as he liked
to call God, the Father) was calling him to China. As
events turned out, all doors which would have led to China
were closed one after the other: it seemed that God had an
altogether different plan for Peter Marshall.

At this juncture his cousin, Jim Broadbent, was led to
present to Peter the idea of his emigrating to the United
States to enter the ministry. The young Scot was stubbornly
resistant to his cousin's suggestion but agreed to pray
about it.

Three weeks later Peter still had no answer. Then
one Sunday afternoon as he was walking through a
rhododendron-lined lane in the Sholto Douglas Estate, the
Chief gave him his marching orders.

"I was walking along that lane puzzling over the decision
before me," he was to say later, "when all at once I *knew*.
The answer was a clear-cut strong inner conviction, quite
unmistakable, that God wanted me in the United States of
America."

So on April 5, 1927, Peter Marshall arrived at the Bat-
tery off Ellis Island; from there he went to Elizabeth, New
Jersey; then surprisingly, south to Birmingham, Alabama;
to Georgia's Columbia Theological Seminary; from thence
years later, to the Nation's capital where he would become
a major spokesman for the Chief.

"My own choice was to go to China," we college students heard him say that day in Atlanta. "But the Holy
Spirit had other plans. If God is to use us as His hands and
feet and voice, it is just as necessary for Him to guide us
geographically as in any other way. It *does* matter to God
where we are at any given time."

The Spirit cannot guide us, however, as long as we insist
on finding our own way. It is as if we, groping along in the
dark, are offered a powerful lantern to light our path, but

refuse it, preferring to stumble along striking one flickering match after the other.

Instead, first we have to ask the Spirit to lead us; then by an act of will place our life situations and our future in His hands; and then trust that He will get His instructions through to us.

Second, seeking to control everything ourselves by the same kind of wire-pulling and door-crashing practiced by those who know nothing of God's leading, can have no place in the Spirit-led life. Such manipulation merely impedes the Spirit's work on our behalf.

I can affirm from experience that allowing the Helper to guide one's life is an exciting, fulfilling way to live. His plans for each of us are so startlingly superior to anything we can imagine.

HELPFUL READING: Acts 8:26–40

HIS WORD FOR YOU: Formula for a significant life.
Humble yourselves—feeling very insignificant—in the presence of the Lord, and He will exalt you.—He will lift you up and make your lips significant.
(James 4:10, AMPLIFIED)

PRAYER: *Dear Lord, I scarcely understand my own reluctance to take hands off and let You manage my affairs. Do I actually think that You, the sovereign, omnipotent God, cannot get along without my help! Lord, forgive me for presumption like that.*

But sometimes I find it harder to wait on You, being bidden not to do anything at all except trust You, than it would be to rush ahead trying to arrange things myself. I need Your help with this. I ask for patience. Above all, I ask for the faith to believe that my future is important to You.

Thank You that my times are in Your loving hands. Amen.

3   He Protects Me

But safe he lives who listens to me;
from fear of harm he shall be wholly free.

God is to us a God of deliverances and salvation, and to
God, the Lord, belongs escape from death. . . .
    (Proverbs 1:33, MOFFATT; Psalm 68:20, AMPLIFIED)

If we were willing to accept the Spirit's help and to listen
to His voice, many of the evils, difficulties, and accidents
that befall us would be avoided. I believe this to be an
important answer to the question so often asked, "How
could a loving God allow such-and-such a dreadful calam-
ity to happen?"

Across the years I have heard so many true incidents of
escape from death by following the Spirit's instructions
that it is difficult to choose among them. All have this in
common: someone in a crisis situation was able to hear the
Spirit's quiet interior voice and moved to obey, thus escaping death.

One evening over dinner in a New York City restaurant
a friend told this story. . . . Several years previously she and
her two young nephews were aboard a plane at Orly Air-
port (Paris) waiting to take off for London. "As I sat
there," the friend told me, "suddenly that quiet but very
clear and authoritative Voice told me to take my nephews
and deplane at once. No explanation was given. I obeyed
and even managed to get our baggage pulled off." She
paused, looking me directly in the eyes. "That plane
crashed. All aboard perished."

"What a story!" I marveled. "And what courage it took for you to obey that!"

But what about the other passengers, we wonder? One thing we know. God is no respecter of persons. He loved them as much as He loved my friend. Then did the Spirit try to get a message through to one or more mechanics? To the pilot? To other passengers too? No doubt. Though there can be no definitive answer, surely we need to ponder the important interplay between man's free will and the Spirit's mission to guide and protect us.

Another friend, the Reverend Joseph Bishop of Rye, New York, has related this story. . . . For years Joe had befriended and ministered to Ruth, one of his parishioners and a cerebral palsy victim from birth. Ruth could get around only with the aid of an ingeniously equipped, motorized wheelchair built for her by her father. But the crippled body was presided over by a highly gifted mind. With the constant love and encouragement of her family and her pastor, Ruth had graduated from Drew University.

Several years followed, with Ruth helping with the church's weekday Nursery School. But Ruthie's greatest longing was to be able to hold a regular job, earn her own way in the world. In her case, since she had difficulty even feeding herself, her dream seemed impossible of attainment.

Late one afternoon Joe was returning home from his church office. At his front steps the Spirit spoke to him. It was "a compelling, irresistible, mandatory call to go to see Ruthie. I had not planned to do so." Yet down to her house he strode as fast as he could walk.

Joe let himself in by the side entrance and called out Ruthie's name. He found her in a back room weeping and alone. Ruth had been in deep depression with feelings of suicide.

That afternoon both Ruth and Joe found themselves stunned, overwhelmed by the realization of God's love and caring. What had begun as a possible tragedy ended up as praise.

Ruth went on to get a Ph.D. at the University of Illinois and is now on the staff of a state hospital in Iowa. God even provided Frances, a devoted, mentally limited companion, to care for her. Frances needed Ruth's fine mind and Ruth needed Frances's strong arms and legs.

Such true stories dramatize for us how one's survival can depend upon our receiving into our hearts the Helper. At the moment of being "born again," each of us is given the ears in our spirit (a new receiving set) to enable us to hear His voice. But it's as if the receiving set is faultily connected up and is bringing in intermittent messages with much static and dead air until we have received the infilling of the Spirit.

We need to practice listening and obeying in the daily round. Only then will we be prepared to hear His directions for crisis situations.

HELPFUL READING: Acts 16:6, 7; 22:17–21

HIS WORD FOR YOU: The Lord helps and delivers in time of trouble.

When you pass through the waters I will be with you, and through the rivers they shall not overwhelm you; when you walk through the fire you shall not be burned or scorched, nor shall the flame kindle upon you.
(Isaiah 43:2, AMPLIFIED)

PRAYER: *Dear God, You are my Father, I am Your child. I put my hand in Yours, thanking You that Your will is to keep me safely until my work is completed here. Thank You for the tender care that would speak to me through the Holy Spirit. I do so want to learn how to hear and to be obedient. Open my ears of the spirit. Remind me to listen many times a day. And oh Lord, give me an obedient heart. In Jesus' name, I pray. Amen.*

4 *He Is with Me in Everyday Situations*

Likewise the Spirit helps us in our weakness.
(Romans 8:26, RSV)

The literal rendering of the Greek word *Paraclete* can be interpreted variously as "One at hand" or as "One by our side" . . . "One alongside to help" . . . "One who may be counted upon in any emergency."

Jesus' succinct statement of our human plight tells us clearly enough why we so desperately need the Holy Spirit as Helper:

Apart from Me—cut off from vital union with Me—you can do nothing.[1] Jn. 15:5

Actually, when we human beings feel most capable of handling life on our own, invariably that is when we are most in need of Jesus' help mediated to us by the Spirit. Nor is this just spiritual need. It is a practical, workaday assistance that the Helper longs to give us.

One day I was trying to copy a magazine picture of an attractive hour-glass-shaped curtain for the glass in our kitchen door. It looked easy. But in vain I labored over the fabric for three hours, growing more frustrated, baffled, and irritated by the minute.

Challenged by my failure, I then called in a friend, only to find that she too was unable to come up with a workable pattern. Finally, I decided to give up the whole project. Thereupon I turned to other household tasks.

At that point, very quietly, the Helper took over. "Do it this way," He told me, and proceeded to give me simple, practical instructions in the form of a series of pictures in my mind. The technique He suggested had not once occurred either to me or to my friend. It worked easily, perfectly.

Some of the Spirit's help is also aimed at releasing us from many of the time-consuming details of daily life—not to make us lazy, but so that we can be free to take on more important tasks for Him and to help other people. Indeed, when we allow the Spirit to move through us to the needs of others, we are going to be so busy as sorely to need the Spirit's very practical help—finding where to repair an important tool, locating a misplaced article, or saving money on food or clothing purchases.

One day I felt a nudging to take a particular book to a next-door neighbor who was in bondage to fears of all kinds. But the Helper said quietly, "There is no need to take it over right now. Wait a while, and she will come to you."

So I turned to other tasks. Within an hour the neighbor appeared at our front door. I gave her the book and discovered that she had in hand a recipe for a special dish I had been wanting to make.

The time and effort saved in such experiences would be a gift enough. But there is also immense joy and exhilaration and faith-building in these hourly, daily demonstrations of the Helper's presence—God "tabernacling with us."

HELPFUL READING: Matthew 10:29–31; 17:24–27

HIS WORD FOR YOU: Our every need will be met.
And my God will liberally supply (fill to the full) your every need according to His riches in glory in Christ Jesus.

(Philippians 4:19, AMPLIFIED)

PRAYER: *Dear Lord, that You should be interested in every detail of my everyday life seems almost too good to be true—and yet too wonderful not to be true. I have sorely needed Your reassurance about this. You know how often I've wondered whether I should bother the Lord of the universe with the trivia of my little life. Now I accept Your word that the fabric of daily life is woven of such details and trivia, and that how I handle this is important to You and to the kingdom. And since You are concerned with the fall of each sparrow, how much more are You concerned about me! How I thank you, Lord! Amen.*

5 *He Is My Remembrancer*

But the Counselor, the Holy Spirit, whom the Father will send in my name, he will teach you all things, and bring to your remembrance all that I have said to you.
(John 14:26, RSV)

The early days of my walk in the Spirit were full of exciting discoveries. After all, the gospel narratives are startlingly brief. There is so much *not* told us, so many gaps. Mostly, we are given principles as guidelines, but the question always is, how does this work out in everyday life? How do I apply this in my workaday world?

Jesus' words about the Spirit teaching us all things and bringing to our remembrance all that Jesus has said, are one such guideline. My exciting discovery was that Jesus' promise is much more inclusive than we have thought or dreamed. Once started on my walk in the Spirit, I found that the Helper had quietly become the living Repository of my memory and my mind—that incredibly intricate human brain that still baffles all scientists—the Chief Librarian of my lifetime storehouse of memories, thoughts, quotations, all kinds of specific data.

He was now in charge of the whole, and I could trust Him to find and bring up out of the voluminous "stacks" of memory whatever I needed. There were those everyday gaps in memory when I could not recall a person's name or the name of a street or a book or a verse of Scripture. The Spirit was eager to come to my assistance. When I asked Him for this help and then released the problem from my mind, usually not immediately, but within hours, the Helper would deliver the answer.

Then I experienced His delight in showing me what to do about misplaced articles for which I was hunting.

Subsequently, I came upon yet another facet of the helper's role as our Remembrancer. This is pointed out in Jesus' promise that when we are . . .

> brought before kings and governors for my name's sake . . . Settle it therefore in your minds, not to meditate beforehand how to answer; for I will give you a mouth and wisdom, which none of your adversaries will be able to withstand or contradict.[1]

LK 21. 12-15

Though the promise refers specifically to the crisis situations of Christians caught in persecution, an experience in the summer of 1963 showed me how all-inclusive this promise is too.

It happened towards the end of a trip through the South Seas to Australia. The British Commonwealth edition of my book *Beyond Our Selves* had just been released, and I had been asked to make some bookstore, press, and television appearances in Sydney and Melbourne. Among these was the televised program "Meet The Press" seen all over Australia and noted for its tough approach.

No hint of the questions was allowed ahead of time. The visitor faced a panel of press men and women who could ask anything they wished, and who had acquired a reputation for ruthlessness. I sensed that my husband Leonard (we had been married in 1959, ten years after Peter's death) and several friends who had accompanied me to the studio and who would be monitoring the program in a private room, were afraid for me. They knew that as an author, I am a "paper person" always with a pencil in hand. And paper people are rarely noted for carrying specifics in their heads. So how would I fare since no notes could be used or referred to on "Meet the Press"?

Before the program began, quietly—within myself—I asked the Helper to take over. "This panel isn't exactly 'kings and governors,' " I told Him, "but they might as well be. Since there's no way I can meditate beforehand on how to answer, this is the perfect setup for You to handle. I am helpless; You are adequate. Please manage everything for me."

And He did! Never have I had a prayer more gloriously answered. The first part of the answer was that the representatives of the press were not antagonistic. But on top of that, the Helper revealed Himself a brilliant Rememberer. I heard myself calmly giving dates, place names, quoting portions of Peter Marshall's Senate prayers verbatim, even (most surprising of all) providing some sports data—I, who pay little attention to professional sports!

So I could never doubt that this was all the Spirit's work. Such relaxation and exuberance entered in, that my time with "Meet the Press" became pure joy all the way—fun for me and for the interviewers.

Try the Helper as Your Remembrancer. Experiment with small, everyday needs first. As you learn how adequate and trustworthy He is, as you relax and trust Him more and more, you will find Him a Companion of inestimable worth.

How did we ever live without Him!

HELPFUL READING: I John 2:24–29

HIS WORD FOR YOU: Our wonderful burden-bearing Lord!

> *Blessed be the Lord, Who bears our burdens and carries us day by day, even the God Who is our salvation!*
> (Psalm 68:19, AMPLIFIED)

PRAYER: *Lord, I confess that I have been reluctant to admit You into my daily life in relation to small, intimate needs. I had not thought that the Lord of the universe, high and lifted up, should be bothered with my little problems. Yet here You are making it clear to us that the Helper will be as close to us as our own thoughts, supplying even needed information and reminding us in a critical moment of Your words of promise and blessing.*

Thank You too for putting Your finger so incisively on a deeper reason for my reluctance to admit You to the minutiae of my life. I have been afraid of the fair exchange You are asking of me: the Helper will supply everything—even these small needs—in exchange for my whole life. Not only does He want to use me, He wants an exuberance of giving on both sides.

Lord, melt away any pockets of resistance left. Don't let me hug any part of my life to myself.

Show me today how to take at least one definite step of trusting the Helper. Thank You, Lord. Amen.

6 He Gives Me New Desires

And all of us . . . are constantly being transfigured into His very own image in ever increasing splendor and from one degree of Glory to another; [for this comes] from the Lord [Who is] the Spirit.

(II Corinthians 3:18, AMPLIFIED)

The Helper can indeed change our desires and our tastes and our habit patterns.

Some years ago I had a friend in Washington, D.C., Winifred Hanigan, who had established a unique dress business. For a yearly fee, she would consult with a client about her clothing needs for her life-style, then handle all shopping and fitting for her. Since the nation's capital is full of small-town people in need of sudden sophistication, Winifred's service was a godsend to wives of officialdom and the diplomatic service.

Janet was a friend of mine, a Kansas girl working on Capitol Hill. She knew that she was hopelessly deficient in clothing taste and know-how, yet she did not have Winifred's fee. Our friend took Janet on anyway.

The first concern was acquiring basics. A necessary basic for Janet's job and the Washington climate, Winifred told her protégé, was a fine three-piece tweed outfit—suit and coat. A beautiful British tweed, mostly in deep reds, was selected and ordered.

When it arrived and Janet picked up the outfit, she cried all the way from Winifred's shop to the bus stop on Connecticut Avenue. The tweeds were ridiculously expensive. They cost all of Janet's salary for two weeks. And she wasn't even sure she *liked* the outfit!

Then we watched a strange thing happen. As Janet wore the clothes made of the beautiful tweed, she noticed her own taste being transformed. The purchase turned out to be one of the mainstays of Janet's wardrobe for eight years. The tweeds were not worn out even then.

But all this could not have happened without Janet putting herself in Winifred's hands, trusting her enough to obey her.

This is a homely illustration, an analogy of the process by which the Spirit changes us. But He can't do this until we trust Him enough to put ourselves in His hands. . . . "For all who are led by the Spirit of God are sons of God," Paul solemnly tells us.[1] *Ro. 8:14*

Then immediately Paul points out that this does not mean "a spirit of slavery to put you once more in bondage to fear. . . ." Rather, this is "sonship—in the bliss of which we cry, Abba! . . . Father!"[2] *Ro. 8:15*

When Janet submitted herself and her taste to Winifred, exactly as a son or daughter submits to a parent, then an astonishing process was set in motion: her taste was "transformed . . . by the . . . renewal of [her] mind—by its new ideals and its new attitude. . . ."[3] And this is exactly the way the Spirit deals with us when we submit ourselves as sons. *Ro. 12:2*

Further, just as Janet found that she could trust Winifred's taste, even so we find the Spirit possesses the kind of taste that we can trust implicitly.

We have only to look around us at the beauties He wrought as One of the Agents in the creation of our world to know that here is One of impeccable taste, our world's finest Connoisseur. Anywhere we turn in nature we see the demonstration of this—from the lowliest roadside buttercup to the intricately engineered iridescence of seashells like the chambered nautilus or the Pacific triton's trumpet; from the proud beauty of the preening male cardinal to the flashing brilliance of the tiny hummingbirds; in every foaming, curling wave of the ocean and every star in the sky.

True, in ourselves we are not quite ready for such perfection. At points each of us wants to drag along in the mud of mediocrity. Our taste has to be educated upwards as Janet's had to be. But we have nothing to fear in this process.

We can trust the Spirit in His work of renewing and transforming us into sons and daughters fit for the King.

HELPFUL READING: Ephesians 4:22–32

HIS WORD FOR YOU: God finishes what He began.
The Lord will perfect that which concerns me: thy mercy, O Lord, endures forever: forsake not the works of Your own hands.
(Psalm 138:8, AMPLIFIED)

PRAYER: *Lord, I sense that I haven't even begun to grasp the extent of the transformation You want to make in me. Yet I thank You that these changes do not mean that I will be any less myself. I begin to see that it's rather my tendency "to be conformed to the world" that blurs and all but wipes out my individuality. Your "transforming" enhances the real me.*

Lord, by an act of will, I ask You to undertake on my behalf that transformation. Give me the ability and the grace to be quick to hear, to bend with the wind of the Spirit, to obey. In Jesus' name. Amen.

7 He Changes My Undesirable Habit Patterns

I indeed baptize you with water unto repentance: but he that cometh after me . . . shall baptize you with the Holy Ghost and with fire.

. . . that we . . . might walk in newness of life.
    (Matthew 3:11, KJV; Romans 6:4, RSV)

It is as *sinners* that we receive Christ for salvation and are baptized in water. It is then as *sons* that we receive the baptism of the Spirit. Notice how clearly John the Baptist (as quoted by Matthew above) makes this distinction. After we have been received by Jesus and are then heirs of the Father, along with Him, then Jesus Himself (He alone) can baptize us with the Spirit. Not until we have entered into both of these experiences can we walk in full newness of life. Our "born again" life is never our own natural life raised to its highest development. Rather, it is that life scrapped, dead, "crucified with Christ." Then to take the place of that old natural life, the Divine life condescends to its lowliest home—your heart and mine. Until the Spirit is thus tabernacling with us, the newness of life of which the Apostle Paul so often spoke will be mere theory and will elude us.

But once we have been born again and have received the Spirit, then what is the newness of life like? What can we expect?

Some of the changes involve deep and extensive inner

transformation. Study the fifth chapter of Galatians and note the element of change which Paul depicts and his list of high character traits which should be common to all who receive the Spirit: love, a great joy and gladness, an even-temper and patience, kindness and a generosity in our judgment of our fellows, faithfulness (hanging in there), gentleness, self-control and self-restraint.[1] *Gal. 5:22, 23*

When we allow the Spirit to develop in us these gracious traits, then like the boy Jesus growing up, we too will "increase in wisdom . . . and in favor with God and man."[2] *Lk. 2:52*

Other changes the Helper will make in us will then vary from person to person. Some will be more superficial, yet specific and noticeable changes in tastes and in habit patterns. One girl, who had been barely tolerant of other people's pets, found herself loving dogs. Another lost her taste for heavy makeup. Yet another, who had often gone to see X-rated movies (especially foreign ones), now found these distasteful to her.

A man was no longer interested in escaping into reading detective stories for interminable hours. Another man, a compulsive viewer of televised sports, found this of sharply decreasing importance to him. An Atlanta friend who for years had habitually looked forward to his late-afternoon bourbon and water was astonished to find himself not wanting the drink.

In His changing of our desire-world the Spirit will deal with each of us differently. Given that, any church or religious group that seeks to place us back "under law" with lists of "Thou shalt nots" is denying the Spirit's work and interfering with it.

We watched the unique individuality of the Spirit's work with our friend Betty in Delray Beach, Florida. For years she had been struggling to stop smoking. She felt convicted about a child of the King being in bondage to some grains of tobacco wrapped in a paper tube. Yet Betty felt helpless to get free of this and was therefore discouraged.

One night she had a short vivid dream. She saw the face of the speaker at a recent meeting who had mentioned the smoking problem. Then a hand and arm with a lighted cigarette between the fingers came into view. In the dream the fingers began vigorously tamping out the cigarette. There the dream ended.

The next morning the dream was still vividly present to Betty. She wondered if its meaning could be as obvious as it seemed. Pondering this, she automatically reached for her package of cigarettes. A single cigarette was left in the package. Betty lighted it, but she soon found that it tasted different—not at all good. With disgust she tamped the cigarette out exactly as in the dream. She has had no desire to smoke since.

This is the gracious work of the Spirit.

HELPFUL READING: Galatians 5:16–24

HIS WORD FOR YOU: A prescription for getting rid of a bad habit.

But this shall be the covenant that I will make with the house of Israel; After those days, saith the Lord, I will put my law in their inward parts, and write it in their hearts. . . .

(Jeremiah 31:33, KJV)

PRAYER: *Lord Jesus, how I thank You that the freedom into which You call me does not seek to change me by forcing me to do what I do not want to do, rather changes me on the inside by giving me new desires. Only a love like Yours could ever have thought of such a gracious plan. For I find it no burden to do what my new desires want to do.*

So I open myself to You and give You permission to change me as it pleases You. Lord, I anticipate the adventure that lies ahead. Thank You, Lord, thank You. Amen.

Part Four

How the Helper Ministers to Me at a Deep Level

1 *He Convicts Me of Sin*

If I go, I will send him [the Helper] to you. And when he comes, he will convince the world concerning sin . . . because they do not believe in me. . . .
(John 16:7–9, RSV)

If a group of knowledgeable Christians were asked, "By what signs can one recognize that he has just received the Spirit?" we might get a variety of answers: "I felt a great inrush of love and joy," or, "My whole body tingled with a great warmth; I wanted to shout—and did," or, "I spoke in a heavenly language for the first time."

Yet the answer Jesus gave to His apostles during His Last Supper talk was altogether different: "When the Helper comes, He will convict the world of sin."

Why, we wonder, since Jesus was sending the Spirit to help us and to be our Comforter, would the Spirit's first priority be to convict us of sin? That sounds so stringent, anything but comforting.

And what sin did He mean? When we speak of sin, we think of lying, cheating, greed, slander, a vicious tongue, temper, cruelty, sexual promiscuity, adultery, murder and the like, whereas, when Jesus spoke of the convicting work of the Holy Spirit, He did not mention those sins. In fact, He used the singular "sin," then went on to define sin as unbelief—"Because they do not believe in me."

Jesus' viewpoint here is clearly not ours, since most of us rarely think of unbelief as being sin. In fact, sometimes we are actually proud of it, calling unbelief resistance to superstition and foolish credulity, thinking of our skepticism as sophistication, the result of our being educated out of prejudice—the blind acceptance of unproven premises.

At best, we view unbelief as a disability we really can't help—"I'm sorry, I wish I could believe. But you know I have to be honest. After all, I can't work faith up in myself."

Neither sinking down before unbelief helplessly nor bowing before it in intellectual pride solves our problem here. In both instances we are left exactly where we were before.

Then why does Scripture not only call unbelief a sin, but the fountainhead of all sin, the sin that encompasses all other sins?

Because by our unbelief we reject Jesus Christ, who He is, all He stands for, what He came to earth to do.

It was of this root sin that the Spirit convicted three thousand men on the Day of Pentecost through the second sermon Simon Peter ever preached. Bluntly, Peter had charged them with rejecting the Lord of Life—"whom you crucified and killed by the hands of lawless men." Whereupon they were "cut to the heart" and anxiously inquired, "Brethren, what shall we do?"[1]

How often I have heard preachers tell their congregations that we today "crucify the Lord afresh." This same thought is also in that lovely spiritual, "Were You There When They Crucified My Lord?"

Yet until recently something about that thought eluded me. Then the Spirit showed me that every time I reject Jesus' ability to handle any problem or problem area of my life, I am rejecting Him as the Lord of Life as truly as did the three thousand on the Day of Pentecost. He claimed to be the Savior, to be able to save us from any sin, any bondage, any problem. By disclaiming that, with regard to any one of my problems, I am calling Jesus a liar and a charlatan—a fake prophet—as truly as did those who long ago howled for His death before Pilate and who drove in the nails.

At that point I am also back in the Garden of Eden standing beside Adam and Eve giving heed to the serpent —"Don't believe God. He's really trying to deceive you and take away your happiness. After all, you know your own situation best. Don't be afraid to follow your own best judgment."

Whenever I follow the serpent's twisted, convoluted advice, instantly I reveal the root of my sin-nature. It has many tentacles, among them my rebellion against God, the self-will of my determination to have my own way, and my arrogance. How ridiculous we human beings are when we set the pathetic limitations of our finite minds and petty judgment over against the infinite wisdom of our Creator! We can see this in regard to our own children. We can simply judge better than they can. . . . "No, you may *not* ride your bike in the heavy traffic downtown." . . . "Stop it, Johnny, you'll pull that chest over on yourself." . . . "Debbie, *no!* You cannot play with matches." But how blind we are to the fact that we grownups are in an even more untenable position in relation to our Heavenly Father.

Even so, we hear our amazing Lord telling us, "Neither do I condemn you." Here too, His viewpoint is very different from ours. Even as we are inclined to center down on legalistic and fleshly sins, so we usually assume that we are in for massive doses of judgment and condemnation.

Not so!

For God sent the Son into the world, not to condemn the world, but that the world might be saved through him.[2] Jn 3:17

The difference here is that we think of sin as the breaking of laws, whereas Jesus thinks of sin as being bound. Why would anyone with goodwill condemn a poor man bound with chains or tied with heavy rope? Would he not rather want to free him?

That, Scripture tells us, is the plight of us all before we meet Jesus because

All have sinned. . . .
   If we say we have no sin, we deceive ourselves,
   and the truth is not in us.

Ro. 3:23
I Jn 1:8
Jn 8:34

Every one who commits sin is a slave to sin.[3]

And Jesus came to earth, He announced at the beginning of His public ministry, for the express purpose not of condemning us, but of releasing all of us sin-captives.[4] Lk 4:18

Therefore, until we see ourselves as bound in many specific areas and in need of freeing and saving, obviously we will have no need of the Savior. Our danger then will be that of approaching Jesus not as a Savior but as a Santa Claus for the good gifts He can give us.

The truth is that none of us can go anywhere in the

Christian life so long as we are chained with unbelief. For in any area we look, until we believe that Jesus is the Savior of our life for whatever our problem is—health or sex or money or job or strained or severed human relationships or whatever—there is nothing He can do for us. And we will then stay bound on a level plateau, getting nowhere until the Spirit convicts us too of unbelief as the sin it is, until we begin to see God's grief for our lack of trust in the Lord of life, and allow Jesus to deal with this sin in as summary a fashion as He deals with all sin.

So long have most of us thought fuzzily about unbelief that there is relief in knowing of this clear-cut remedy for our sin. The steps are clear: we must stop all excuses; confess our lack of trusting Jesus as sin; give the Spirit permission to bring us to repentance about this, even at the emotional level; claim God's promise of forgiveness and cleansing.[5]

Then, to our delight, we shall find a fresh and new faith springing up in us like the bubbling up of a spring of clear water.

HELPFUL READING: Acts 2:14–21.

HIS WORD FOR YOU: Jesus—God's eternal "Yes."

For all the promises of God find their Yes in Him [Christ].

(II Corinthians 1:20, RSV)

PRAYER: *Lord Jesus, Sovereign Lord, into whose hands the Father has given all power, I lift up my heart and my life to You.*

Lord, so often I must have grieved You with my lack of trust. Your loving, giving heart has wanted to shower good gifts on me and my family and friends, yet I have been too bound by the sin of not believing even to lift my hands to receive the gifts.

Lord Jesus, forgive me!

I do confess my unbelief as the sin it is. And I ask You now to forgive me and to cleanse me of this black sin. I thank You that the "cleansing from all unrighteousness" You have promised includes the gift of Your own implicit trust in the goodness, the mercy, and the present-day power of the Father.

Thank You, Lord. Amen.

2 *He Values My Personhood*

Now the Lord is that Spirit; and where the Spirit of the Lord is, there is liberty.

(II Corinthians 3:17, KJV)

Many people are afraid of the Helper. Often unspoken is the fear, "If I assent to the Spirit, won't He then just take over and make me do all sorts of kooky things?"

But from a great pool of Christian experience comes the answer. No, the Helper never violates anyone's free will. He, like each person of the Trinity, has supreme respect for our personhood. He will never trample upon that or take us any further than we are willing to go.

In this regard the Holy Spirit and all powers of darkness stand in complete antithesis. Satan despises our personhood and steadily seeks to suck all freedom of will from us. Satan wants us in slavery to him; the Helper wants our freedom.

This is at once an awesome measure both of the value that God places upon the creatures made in His own image and of the humility of Jesus who "stooped low, made himself of no reputation, and took upon him the form of a servant."[1] Phil 2:7

The Spirit faithfully reflects both attributes here: (1) the freedom of choice of the human will is one of the most precious gifts God has given us. Therefore, the Helper waits upon the assent of our will. And, (2) in line with Jesus' own humility, the Helper waits to see how much welcome we will accord Him; how open we are to His help, so that through us He can help others. This amazing humility means that the Spirit actually puts Himself at the disposal of our volition. In that sense, He even submits Himself to our human weakness and frailty.

The supreme value Jesus places on our freedom of will was dramatized for me during my encounter with the Risen Lord that memorable night, September 14, 1943, at my parents' home in Seaview, Virginia.

I had already been ill many months, and was not getting better. Discouragement was deep. Before falling asleep, I had given up my own struggle for healing. I had already tried everything. Nothing had worked. So with many tears, I cast myself on the mercy of God. The relinquishment was complete.

At about 3:30 A.M. I was awakened from a sound sleep —very wide awake. Suddenly—He was there. Jesus, standing on the right side of the bed. The room crackled and vibrated.

Since I have detailed this experience elsewhere, I want to emphasize here just one aspect of the electrifying moments that followed. At the end, Jesus gave me this simple directive, "Go, and tell your mother."

Even in that moment of command, I was acutely aware of Jesus' regard for my personhood and of His hands-off attitude as regards my free will. There was no stampeding, no crowding. The choice to obey or not to obey was clearly mine. That's the way Jesus wanted it to be.

In a flash, I understood how it had been with that rich young ruler in the gospels. . . . "Go, and sell what you have . . . and follow Me." With him too, as with me that night, there had been Jesus' hands-off attitude, "You decide." Mark's account of this incident tells us that Jesus beholding the young man, loved him.[2] Even so, Jesus had stood silently by, love in His eyes, yet had watched the young man turn his back and walk away. MK 10:21

Not understanding why He wanted me to tell my mother, I still knew that I must obey anyway. My healing began at that point of blind obedience. In retrospect, I realized that it was not for my mother's sake that Jesus had given me this directive, but for my own sake: I had to bend the will and obey.

Since that night I have understood that this reverence for the freedom of life God Himself has given us is a position neither the Father, nor Jesus, the Son, nor the Spirit will ever abdicate.

So what does this mean in our walk with the Helper?

The startling truth is that He will come to us and fill us only to the degree that we are willing to be filled. He insists upon being a welcome guest in our hearts and beings, never a trespasser or an interloper or a squatter.

In fact, we can, whenever we choose, turn this sympathetic, courteous Guest from the door of our heart. We can also so grieve Him with wrong attitudes that He simply withdraws. . . .[3] *Eph 4:25-32*

When the truth of this final humility of God dawns upon us, it puts an end to any fear about losing our selfhood to the Helper.

It also places a fearsome responsibility upon *us*. How much do we want Him? How much of Him are we willing to receive? What limitations are we placing upon Him?

It follows that even after our initial baptism of the Spirit, as our willingness and receptivity increase, we will also experience repeated fillings. These will come as we step out in ministry. Special filling and special outpouring will be given for tough situations, extremities we alone could never handle. This has been the experience of many individuals across the centuries.

HELPFUL READING: Matthew 19:16–22

HIS WORD FOR YOU: Take a deep breath of the fresh wind of the Spirit.

> *The Spirit of the Lord is upon me, because the Lord has anointed me . . . to proclaim liberty to the captives . . . to grant a garland of beauty instead of ashes, the oil of joy for mourning, the garment of praise instead of a heavy, burdened and failing spirit. . . .*
>
> *Everlasting joy shall be theirs.*
>   (Isaiah 61:1, 3, 7, AMPLIFIED)

PRAYER: *Lord, I see now that my fear of the Spirit has also, in an odd way, been a dodge for placing the responsibility of my life and growth on You rather than seeing that the degree of my openness to You rests squarely on my shoulders. Often I have deceived myself—"Whatever God wants to give me, it's up to Him"—when all the time, the door of my heart was shut, with most of the shutters drawn.*

Lord, thank You for always knocking on the door and never crashing it down. Lord, Helper, it is my will to open the door wide to You. Enter, Lord, and be my honored Guest. What joy to welcome and receive You! Amen.

3 He Teaches Me about Tears

And I will give them . . . a new heart—and I will put a new spirit within them; and I will take the stony [unnaturally hardened] heart out of their flesh, and will give them a heart of flesh [sensitive and responsive to the touch of their God].

(Ezekiel 11:19, AMPLIFIED)

Jack is a fine professional man with serious family problems. He has many Christian friends who love him and his family and who want to help. Yet Jack is trying to carry his heavy burden all alone, the stiff-upper-lip way. Why, we have wondered, does he insist upon isolating himself? Why will he not ever unburden his heart and mind when he needs to so desperately?

Then one day I found out why. "I was reared an Anglican," Jack told me. "Pretty starchy, I guess. I'd like to come and see you and your husband. Honestly, I would. But I know I couldn't do it without getting emotional—*and that just wouldn't do.*"

I looked at Jack in astonishment. He would actually then pass up the talk-therapy and the prayer-therapy needed because he was afraid of tears!

An incident like this dramatizes how warped our values can become and how completely we have misunderstood about tears for men as well as women. The Spirit would teach us that tears are the pearls of God's kingdom.

Some years ago a close friend, whom I'll call Sam, asked for and received the gift of the Helper in his life. Sam had

always been mistrustful of any emot⋯
religion. His father had been a dignifie⋯
In Sam's house the emphasis had alwa⋯
intellectual approach to Christianity.⋯
School or evangelistic-type hymns were⋯
Sam's taste.

But after the Helper came into Sam's ⋯
we noticed a startling change: anytime our ⋯ ⋯ke of
Jesus, we would see tears in his eyes. Sudden⋯ for the first
time, Jesus was a Person. Not only that, a dear Person.

Nor was Sam embarrassed or apologetic about the mois-
ture in his eyes, though sometimes he would laugh at himself a bit. But Sam knew that something had changed him
down deep at the heart-level. The hardness there before
had been softened, "made responsive to the touch of God,"
as the prophet Ezekiel expressed it. And Sam knew that he
could be glad about tears like those.

Scripture often warns us that a hard heart is the sign of
major trouble between us and God. Our eternal spirit is
then in real jeopardy . . .

Jesus told us that hardness of heart is the major cause
of divorce.[1] *Mt 19:8*

It had been hardness of heart that kept the Israelites
wandering in the desert for forty years, and cost the
entire generation that left Egypt the Promised Land.[2]
Ps. 95:8   Heb 3:7-11

We are warned that toying with sin or deliberately
harboring even small sins in our lives results in an
accretion of the hardening process in us.[3] *Heb 3:13*
Eph. 4:17, 30-32

Jesus made it clear that even for the "good people"
the pride of self-righteousness results in serious hardening of the heart.[4] *Mk 3:5, 8-17   Ro 2:1-5*

This hardening process then, should be something to
fear above all else. And the opposite of this stony heart is
the warm heart of flesh that the Spirit puts within us. The
warm heart is going to result in tears sometimes—
unashamed, unabashed—because now we recognize the
Source.

It was true for Jesus, and He is our pattern here as in all
things. . . .

over the city of Jerusalem because it was a filled with hatred and violence, not knowing the things that belonged to its peace.[5] LK 19:41, 42

He wept at the tomb of his friend Lazarus out of sympathy for His dear friends.[6] Jn 11:34-36

Indeed, as we begin to live and to walk in the Spirit, we find that quite often tears precede some of God's greatest miracles. In such instances, the tears are the evidence that the Spirit is there, moving in power.

Four-year-old Troy Mitchell of Ontario, Canada,[7] had been born with eczema and a chronic asthmatic lung condition. The best medical care available had still not handled the running, oozing sores and cracked lesions resulting from the eczema.

In 1968–69 there had been miraculous healings among several of the Mitchells' friends when they had gone to Kathryn Kuhlman's services in Pittsburgh. Troy's parents and grandparents decided to drive the little boy the five hundred miles to Pittsburgh.

The group got to the auditorium about 9:00 A.M., two hours before the service would begin, and almost immediately, Sharon, Troy's mother, began to weep—for no particular reason. After the service began at eleven, Sharon was crying harder than ever, to the embarrassment of those with her.

Midway through the service, Miss Kuhlman stopped and said, "Someone here is being cured of eczema."

The Canadian group paid no attention. They did not connect this with Troy at all. Sharon continued to weep.

Ten minutes later, Kathryn held up her hand again, "I'm going to have to stop this service yet again. Someone here is grieving the Holy Spirit."

Maggie Hartner, Miss Kuhlman's observant helper, was walking the aisles. She stopped beside the Canadians and asked who they were praying for and what was wrong. When eczema was mentioned, she exclaimed, "Well, for goodness' sake. I've been hunting you all over the auditorium. *Haven't you heard what's been going on?* Please check your child."

Sharon's tears stopped instantly. She jerked Troy's shirt over his head. Every sore on his body was healed. The scabs had turned to powder and dusted to the floor. Even an especially bad draining sore on his left arm was covered with fresh skin.

Troy has never had a return of the eczema. His two Ontario doctors, Doctors Montgomery and McLeod, have both documented the healing.

Sharon's tears, which she had not understood at all, had been the Spirit's insignia, the sign that He was present and at work.

Admittedly, there is weeping that is not of the Spirit, just of the soul or the emotion—tears of rage, of frustration, of self-pity, or as a bid for attention. But very soon we come to know the difference and to value honest emotion as a sign of a heart in which the Helper dwells.

HELPFUL READING: Romans 12:15, 16; Hebrews 3:7–19

HIS WORD FOR YOU: A bright promise for the depressed.

But God, Who comforts and encourages and refreshes and cheers the depressed and the sinking. . . .
(II Corinthians 7:6, AMPLIFIED)

PRAYER: *Lord, I recognize that most of the time my fear of showing emotion is simply pride—silly false pride. This too is a part of self that I would lay on Your altar. Let me never be afraid to mingle my tears with those of my friends and neighbors. If this is the price I pay for a soft, warm, loving heart in which You dwell, then Lord, I pay it gladly, so gladly.*

In Thy name, Amen.

4 He Is My Comforter

As one whom his mother comforteth, so will I comfort you. . . .

And I will pray the Father, and he shall give you another Comforter, that He may abide with you for ever.
(Isaiah 66:13; John 14:16, KJV)

Few of us ever completely outgrow a longing for the comfort of a mother's love when we are hurting. The broken heart can be an open, raw wound. What is dangerous to us and grieves the Spirit above all else is to steel ourselves when emotions well up inside and allow hardness to creep in as a steel-plate protection.

"Let Me handle the hurt for you," the Spirit tells us. There have been many such moments in my life, but one which, though I have written about it before, illustrates best this side of the Helper's tender ministrations to us.

In the early morning hours of January 25, 1949, my husband, Peter Marshall, had awakened with alarming pain in his chest and down both arms. The doctor had come, an ambulance was called, and Peter had been taken to the hospital. I had no way of handling this crisis except to drop on my knees beside the bed.

But my knees no sooner touched the floor than I experienced God as a comforting Mother—something altogether new to me. There was a feeling of the everlasting arms around me and at the same time, waves of tenderness like warm holy oil being poured over me. It was the infinite gentleness of the loving heart of God, more all-pervading than any human mother's love could ever be.

Later was to come the more masculine side of God's caring when He knew that I would need more than tenderness. Then He would give me the first installment of the other side of His comfort—not only loving consolation, but *strength*.

At the moment I interpreted this experience to mean that Peter's heart would be healed. Later, I realized that God had granted this special help so I could understand with a final knowing that He had been with us, a participating Presence through every moment of Peter's homegoing. For at 8:15 that morning, the news came. Peter's heart was forever stilled.

Then it was that I experienced the kind and quality of "comfort" God gives us today through the Holy Spirit. If His comfort were limited to pity or commiserating with us (as much human sympathy is), it would lead us to self-pity—and that's no help at all. Rather, the Spirit's comfort puts courage into us, empowers us to cope with the strains and exigencies of life. The word is *Paraclete*, meaning "alongside, to help in every emergency." And the "comfort" He brings comes from the Latin word *fortis*, meaning "brave." It is a strong, courageous word. Thus the Spirit becomes our "Enabler"—no feather cushion, rather steel in the backbone equal to every sorrow and perplexity and disappointment.

So I found Him in those days following Peter's death. I was not myself. This was not my strength—but the Spirit's. He carried me over and above all circumstances, so that miraculously, *I* could be used to impart strength to a sorrowing congregation and to many in the nation's capital to whom Peter had been a tower of strength.

Yet despite the "fortis" side of God's comfort, I shall always cherish those moments when the Mother-tenderness of God enfolded me.

Years later I would come across passages on this Mother-heart of God in the writings of Hannah W. Smith, the Quaker. In an old book, long out of print, she wrote a lyrical chapter called "The Unselfishness of God" . . .

But now I began to see that if I took all the unselfish love of every mother's heart the whole world over, and piled it all together, and multiplied it by millions, I would still only get a faint idea of the unselfishness of God. . . .

Hannah Smith saw that in the light of this mother-side to God's love for us, even the term "lost" becomes comforting. For . . .

Nothing can be lost that is not owned by somebody, and to be lost means only, not yet found. The lost gold piece is still gold with the image of the King upon it; the lost sheep is a sheep still, not a wolf; the lost son has still the blood of his father in his veins. . . .

Who can imagine a mother with a lost child ever having a ray of comfort until the child is found? Is God then more indifferent than a mother? In fact I believe that all the problems of our spiritual life . . . would vanish like mist before the rising sun, if the full blaze of the mother-heart of God could be turned upon them. . . .

In the Helper we have the perfect balance of God's love—infinite tenderness on the one side, infinite strength on the other. This One with the magnificent dual-sided personality is the Comforter who will be with us forever, every step of the way through this life, no matter what difficulties or sorrows life hands us.

For this we have Jesus' own word. And that never fails!

HELPFUL READING: John 14:26; 16:12–15

HIS WORD FOR YOU: Jesus, our Everlasting Supporter. *It is before his own Master that he stands or falls. And he shall stand and be upheld, for the Master—the Lord —is mighty to support him and make him stand.* (Romans 14:4, AMPLIFIED)

PRAYER: *Father, I thank You that You have so lovingly provided a way to meet my every need, that You and You alone satisfy all the deep and hidden hungers of my heart. You know how much I hurt. You see my unshed tears. I even battle bitterness sometimes, Lord. Take that away and give me Your comfort instead.*

How I praise You for Your gentleness with me. But even more, that You send me the Enabler to supply the strength I do not have, to undertake for me. Thank You, Lord. Thank You. Amen.

5 *He Teaches Me to Pray (I)*

The Spirit himself intercedes for us . . . according to the will of God.

(Romans 8:26, 27, RSV)

Why cannot an omnipotent God, knowing our needs, supply them without waiting for our prayers?

He could, of course, but that is not His plan for his children on earth. Instead, He has dared to arrange it so that He is actually dependent upon us in the sense of our prayers being necessary and all-important to the carrying out of His will on earth.

When Jesus' apostles realized that their prayers were *that* important, they pleaded, "Lord, teach us to pray, as John taught his disciples."[1] *LK 11:1*

Jesus then gave them the Lord's Prayer as the perfect pattern prayer. It is a form (though with immeasurable depths), an outward structure or technique of communicating with the Father.

On the apostles' side, the patterned prayer was all that they were able to receive at that time. Jesus knew that there could be no entering into the full secret of answered prayer until the coming of the Helper.

Looking forward to that great watershed event, during His Last Supper talk their Master spoke especially of the joy of answered prayer ahead:

"Up to this time, you have not asked a . . . thing in My name [that is, presenting all I AM] but now ask and keep on asking and you will receive, so that your joy . . . may be full and complete."[2] *Jn 16:24*

114

"Up to this time" refers to Jesus' imminent glorification and the Helper's coming at Pentecost. At that time God's plan of redemption would be complete: God the Father would receive our petitions at the throne of grace and mercy; the glorified Jesus would be our Advocate and High Priest to present our case and plead our petition before the Father; the Spirit would be the prayer-Helper within us to show us how to prepare our prayer-petitions so that they would be made according to the will of God, and so would always be answered.[3] 1 Jn 5:14

Unquestionably, all of us need massive help with praying aright. So set is our flesh against praying at all that the Helper's first task is to create in us even the basic desire to pray. He is the One who also spotlights for us the prayer-need or topic for prayer by creating a "concern" within us.

Then the Helper has to uncover for us the essence or kernel of what it is we really want. Usually, the true desire at the heart of our prayer-petition is buried under debris that obscures and muddles the real issue.

It is also the Helper's task to show us the blockages in the way of a given prayer-petition—any self-seeking, our desire to control, any resentments and unconfessed sin, etc.

He is also the One who gives us His own prayer faith; also His fervor to replace our tepid love and caring—and so on and on. No wonder we so desperately need the Helper as our prayer Director!

As we recognize our ignorance about praying aright and our helplessness, and actively seek the Spirit's help, our prayer life becomes the anteroom to amazing adventures.

So we have been finding it in a fellowship group of which I have been a member for several years. Doris, a young married woman, a good friend of several in the group, was very ill. The doctors gave little hope.

One evening as Frances, one of the group, was preparing dinner, the Helper spoke to her quietly but urgently, "Doris needs prayer." In her mind's eye Frances could see our entire group of about fourteen people gathered with Doris. Yet she had no idea whether Doris would be willing to receive prayer help.

Frances' obedience however, brought results: two evenings later the whole group gathered. Doris came happily, along with her sister who was visiting her.

Since the Spirit had asked for and engineered the meeting, He was there in power. He brought out into the light Doris' girlhood terror and hurt through her stepfather's sexual abuse. Her sister's presence was necessary to verify all of this and to add details. This childhood trauma had warped Doris' relationship with her husband and with all males and undoubtedly was a factor in producing a serious physical illness.

That evening we watched the Spirit orchestrate through our prayer a beautiful healing of the memories. Jesus lifted from Doris the weight of a lifetime. The evening ended in such glory that we thought Doris' physical problem had also been healed.

Not so. As it turned out, the glory was our loving parting with Doris and her send-off into the next life. She died a month later.

In retrospect, we could only conclude that the Spirit, knowing what lay ahead, was unwilling for Doris to begin her new life encumbered with Satan's wreckage. She went to meet her Lord freed and cleansed and joyous.

All around us are those caught in bondages, imprisoned in fears, hampered by disease to whom Jesus longs to bring His release and His joy. But He waits on *our* prayers. It's a solemn thought.

HELPFUL READING: Acts 9:10–19

HIS WORD FOR YOU: My delight is in Him; His delight is to help me.

Delight yourself also in the Lord, and He will give you the desires and secret petitions of your heart.
    (Psalm 37:4, AMPLIFIED)

PRAYER: *Father, this is the promise I make to You: when the Helper prompts me to pray, I will drop what I'm doing and pray; when I feel a concern for someone, I will talk with You about it and seek Your direction. Keep me alert to the Helper's tug at my sleeve, and give me, Lord, as a gift, a high level of willingness to obey and to follow through.*

I praise You for the gigantic network of prayer and con-

cern and love wrought by the Spirit in us Christians all over the world. I praise You that this stretches even across the barrier of what we call death. I praise You for letting me see the importance of prayer through Your eyes—as the richest resource of the Kingdom, one of the Helper's most treasured gifts to us. Praise You, Lord! Amen.

6   He Teaches Me to Pray (II)

*May the . . . Father grant you the Spirit of wisdom and
revelation . . . illuminating the eyes of your heart so that
you can understand the hope to which He calls us, the
wealth of his glorious heritage in the saints. . . .*
(Ephesians 1:18, 19, MOFFATT)

The Apostle Paul's passionate prayer is that we, God's
people, begin to understand "how rich is the glorious inheritance our Father has bequeathed and stored up for us."
From the moment that we are born again, we have the
right to call Him "Abba, Father," we "who once were no
people and now are God's people."[1] And from that moment on, Paul assures us, all the graces and riches and spiritual treasures and answered prayers we shall ever need in
our lifetime have already been deposited to our account . . .

I Pe. 2:10

Blessing . . . be to the God and Father of our Lord
Jesus Christ . . . Who has blessed us in Christ with
every spiritual [Holy Spirit-given] blessing in the heavenly realm![2]   *Eph 1:3*

There is a good reason why Paul used the past perfect
tense here—God "has blessed us" already—the riches have
already been deposited to our account and are waiting for
us. In our earthly life a son usually has to wait for his
father's death before inheriting the portion of his father's
estate due him. But in the spiritual life, the death that
brought us our inheritance took place two thousand years
ago at Golgotha.

118

When the eyes of the understanding are really opened to see this fact, it altogether changes our prayer life. No longer is there any need of pleading with God to change an undesirable circumstance or to grant us something we need. Since the answer has already been stored up for us, our prayer petition rather needs to be for revelation—"Lord, open my eyes" to see what's there. We are asking Him to let us see at least briefly into the world of spirit, like granting us X-ray eyes for a peep into the treasure room where the golden treasures are stored. Our prayer request is for a sovereign move from the Godward side, *not* in a shifting or change in outward circumstance, but in an inner revelation. From then on, prayer becomes waiting on Him for that insight.

When the insight comes, then faith—"the substance of things not seen"—follows as surely as the sun rises each morning. This "knowing" is altogether different from all pull-yourself-up-by-your-own-bootstraps faith techniques. How often I have tried to quell my own doubts by rebuking negativism and concentrating on the positive—and have tried to call that faith. Yet all such self-help gimmicks are light years away from Jesus' quiet knowing that wrought mighty miracles.

The difference between Jesus and us here is that our Lord seems to have had instant knowing in any particular case because His spiritual eyes were steadily open to revelation. Over and over, patiently, Jesus explained this. . .

> I assure you . . . the Son is able to do nothing from Himself—of His own accord; but He is able to do only what He sees the Father doing. . .[8]

This seeing what the Father is doing is revelation. Or again . . .

> I am able to do nothing from Myself . . . but as I am taught by God and as I get His orders. . . . As the voice comes to Me, so I give a decision. . .[4]

Once again, the hearing and knowing is revelation.

In the life of Jesus, the Gospels give us no instances of miracles until after the Spirit came upon Him at the time of His baptism by John the Baptist. This suggests then that even for the Lord Himself the Spirit was the indispensable

...sus' revelation (followed by His knowing) in
...o the problem before Him—the leper or the blind
...the sick child.

...d Jesus is our perfect pattern, the Pioneer of our faith
here as in all things. So when the Helper lays a concern on
our heart, our part is to ask Him to open our spiritual eyes
and give us the revelation needed.

The next move will then be the Helper's. For us, as for
Jesus, the Helper is the bearer of the needed revelation, the
One who enables us to see the prayer concern as Jesus sees
it. Since the answer to our need is already there, as the
Helper pulls aside the shrouding curtain to reveal to us
what is there, this will necessarily result in faith-knowing.
And at that point the miracle happens.

So our friend Kay Peters discovered some years ago
when her seven-year-old son Don awoke one morning feeling ill.

"Where does it hurt, Don?" his mother asked.

The lad motioned to his jaw and neck. "And here too,"
he said, moving his hands along the inside of his thighs.

Fear gripped Mrs. Peters. Mumps! There was an epi-
demic at his school. Mumps could have dangerous conse-
quences in males!

Kay Peters had prayed many times for people who
needed to be healed—with remarkable results. But as she
started to pray for Don, one thought stopped her—did she
have the right to pray for "natural" childhood diseases?

Immediately, she knew what she had to do—simply ask
Jesus. When she did, the answer was not long in coming:
"Disease is never natural. Health is natural and normal,
what I want for My children. The idea of any childhood
diseases being natural or acceptable is one of Satan's lies,
passed down from generation to generation."

Joy leapt in Kay Peters' heart. Then almost instantly a
counter-thought intruded, as though to knock down the
joy. . . . "Better have mumps now than later."

But why should her son ever have the mumps? Hadn't
Jesus just said—? That couldn't be God's message. The
revelation came—that was Satan! He was telling her not to
believe Jesus. The father of lies had tipped his hand.

Ignoring Satan's negative suggestion, the mother not
only prayed for her son, but added, "And may he be im-
mune from the mumps forever."

With that she received quiet instructions from the inner

Voice: she was not to ask Don how he felt, and she was to observe him carefully.

Very soon it became apparent that the observing was in order that she would miss no part of the miracle. In a few minutes Don began chattering and laughing. Soon he was rolling on the bed. Then he began somersaulting. "Mother, I feel *good*. I don't know *when* I've felt so good! Mother, God heard your prayer and I'm all *well!*"

Don slept soundly that night, and by the next morning there was no trace of soreness or swollen glands. He went on to school that day, and Kay Peters reports that Don, long since a father himself, has never yet had the mumps.

HELPFUL READING: II Kings 6:14–23

HIS WORD FOR YOU: Claim Your Inheritance!

He has granted to us his precious and very great promises, that through these you may escape from the corruption that is in the world because of passion, and become partakers of the divine nature.
(II Peter 1:4, RSV)

PRAYER: *Lord, I have come to You as a beggar believing myself poverty-stricken, lacking, when the fact is I am a child of the King, heir to all Your riches—including every insight and revelation I need for each prayer request. How foolish I must seem to You, Lord! And how my spiritual poverty-complex must grieve You.*

I want so much to sit at the Helper's feet in the School of Prayer and be taught by Him. Show me now how to apply these glorious truths in my own life. And make me a good pupil! In Thy name. Amen.

7 He Convinces Me of Eternal Life

In Him you also . . . were stamped with the seal of the long-promised Holy Spirit.

That [Spirit] is the guarantee of our inheritance—the first fruit, the pledge and foretaste, the down payment on our heritage—in anticipation of its full redemption. . . .
(Ephesians 1:13, 14, AMPLIFIED)

Jesus provided us with few details about life after death. When He gives us the Comforter though, His pledge is that we shall live forever with Him. Furthermore, the Spirit also supplies us with a little foretaste of what that life will be like.

The experience that was my foretaste of immortality occurred in the early morning hours of that September day back in 1943 when suddenly I knew that the Risen Christ was standing beside my bed. The room was charged with electricity, as if the Dynamo of the universe were standing there, as indeed He was!

This was not a vision. I saw nothing with the retina of my eyes. Yet I "saw" every detail clearly with the eyes of the Spirit. In the next few moments I experienced the reality of the spiritual body and learned that it has every faculty of the physical body, though with greater sensitivity and some dimensions added.

There was the total encounter of person to Person. The vividness and impact of Jesus' personality in its myriad facets broke over me like waves cresting on a shore: His kingliness (I wanted to fall on my knees and worship), yet the down-to-earthness of His light touch, His sense of humor, and His loving "You are taking yourself much too seriously. There's nothing here I can't handle."

It was perfectly apparent that He knew every detail of my situation and of the household, as also of my mind and thoughts. He rebuked me for nothing. Rather, the thrust of His personality challenged me out of the physical hole of illness to rise and walk on into the future.

Since that experience, I can never doubt the reality of a life after this one. But now I also understand how essential it is that our inner spirit, so deadened by sin, be touched by the only One who can bring us alive. For how can we enter the next life without our bodies until the faculties of our spiritual body are activated and brought alive?

I also understand better after that night something about what the post-resurrection appearances of Jesus must have been like. I have concluded that our spiritual bodies will have memory (not forgetting anything we know now), mind, will, emotions, personality. I will still be myself. I will know others as themselves, "even as also I am known." There will be nothing shocking in the transition, only a continuation of who I am now.

That memorable night I learned that with my spiritual body there will be instant (and accurate) transferral of thought, words, exchanges from person to person, without the necessity of using the vocal cords or of hearing with the eardrums. In other words, the spiritual body is real, even more real than the physical body.

In the years since that memorable night I have found other ways in which the Spirit is the foretaste and down-payment of immortality. As we begin to live and walk in the Spirit, we find that each wonderful gift He gives us is a sample of that which will be multiplied a thousandfold in the life to come.

There, we shall love as He loves; here, we have a small measure of that love for Him and for each other.

There, we will have the joy of unbroken communion with that amazingly provocative, magnificent Personality; here, only moments and facets of His presence are real to us.

There, we shall have full knowledge; here, the Spirit of Truth gives us bits of knowledge, perception, wisdom, and guidance.

In heaven, there will be no more pain or sickness or disease; here and now, the Spirit sometimes does heal our diseases; upon occasion He is inexplicably blocked from doing so.

There, we shall be done with sorrow; here the Comforter heals our broken hearts and, in the midst of our sorrow, gives us His joy as His pledge of our inheritance.

HELPFUL READING: I Corinthians 15:42–50

HIS WORD FOR YOU: His pledged word, the surety of eternal life.

I assure you, most solemnly I tell you, the person whose ears are open to My words . . . and believes . . . on Him Who sent Me has eternal life. And He does not come into judgment . . . will not come under condemnation— but he has already passed over out of death into life.
(John 5:24, AMPLIFIED)

PRAYER: *My Lord and my God, I thank You that I do not have to wait until death to taste the Spirit's wonderful gifts. I praise You that our immortality begins the minute we ask You to touch us and resurrect our dead spirit. How great it is to have day by day, the Helper's samplings and first fruits of life that will go on and on.*

Give me such fullness of the Spirit as shall make my life here and now, my home and my church, bits of heaven on earth. Amen.

Part Five

The Outpouring of the Helper's Generosity

1 *Joy*

You received the word in much affliction, with joy inspired by the Holy Spirit; so that you became an example to all. . . .

(I Thessalonians 1:6, 7, RSV)

Joy is one of the fruits of the Spirit promised us.[1] Yet perhaps some of us have misunderstood this word. We may think of joy as the exhilaration of prayers being miraculously answered; of the happiness of life going smoothly because of God's blessing on it; or the emotional euphoria of the singing and rejoicing of God's people in invigorating fellowship.

While God often graciously grants us these blessings, the joy of the Spirit is something deeper. The promise is not that the Christian will have only joyous circumstances, but that the Helper will give us the supernatural gift of joy in whatever circumstances we have.

We can see the working out of this in Luke's account of the infant Church. These first Christians had plenty of problems! After Pentecost Peter had no sooner preached his second sermon than he and John were arrested.[2] Following that, a group of apostles were jailed and flogged.[3] Then Stephen was stoned to death.[4] Christians were hunted out and hounded from their homes.[5] James, believed by some scholars to be the Lord's half-brother, was beheaded.[6] Then Peter was imprisoned by Herod, who intended to execute him.[7] And so on and on.

Yet in the midst of all this, the Acts account is peppered with statements about the irrepressible joy of these first Christians. . . . "They partook of their food with gladness."

127

. . . They were ."constantly praising God." . . . "And the disciples were filled with joy and with the Holy Spirit."

And as we watch Paul and Silas being arrested in Philippi, "struck many blows," then thrown into prison with their feet in stocks, to our astonishment we see the Helper's joy taking over in this situation:

> But about midnight, as Paul and Silas were praying
> and singing hymns of praise to God, and the [other]
> prisoners were listening to them. . . .[8] *Acts 16:25*

Those other prisoners must have been listening with incredulity, for there is nothing natural about singing and praising while one's feet are chained in stocks. Obviously, genuine joy in such circumstances is impossible for us humans; it is clearly supernatural.

But Jesus never promised us a gift of human joy delivered to us like a package. Rather, His promise is:

> I [Jesus] have told you these things that *My joy and
> delight may be in you,* and that your joy and gladness
> may be full measure and complete and overflowing.[9] *Jo. 15:11*

It is His own Joy that is pledged us. Through the Spirit, the risen and glorified Lord will Himself take up residence in our cold hearts, and along with Him comes His joy.

Why have we not understood about Jesus' joy? Why has Christendom distorted Scripture by insisting so repeatedly upon the picture of our Lord as "a man of sorrows and acquainted with grief?"

Of course He was *acquainted* with grief since He had come to earth in the flesh for the specific purpose of destroying all of Satan's grief-wreckage. Jesus spent His days going about looking into pain-racked eyes and in summary fashion—with delight—releasing men and women from the enemy's bondages. These were joyous tasks because the Lord of life loathed sickness and disease and broken relationships and insanity and death. So day by day, He left behind a string of victories.

And the greatest victory of all lay ahead—the Cross. Isaiah, in writing of the Messiah to come as being a "man of sorrows and acquainted with grief," was foretelling the agony of that Cross. Yet even there

Jesus . . . for *the joy that was set before Him* endured
the cross. . . .[10] Heb 12:2

And how is it that we have not taken seriously one of the
most beautiful pictures of Jesus in the New Testament? . . .

Thou hast loved righteousness, and hated iniquity;
therefore God, even thy God, *hath anointed thee with
the oil of gladness above thy fellows.*[11] Heb 1:9

So the writer of Hebrews is telling us that Jesus of
Nazareth was possessed of more gladness and more joy
than all other human beings.

But there is even more. Jesus has promised us not just
the extraordinary gladness other men saw in Him while He
walked the earth. We, being supremely blessed by living in
this era of the Holy Spirit, also are pledged the joy of the
victorious, resurrected and glorified Lord.

Looking forward to Pentecost, Jesus said to the eleven
apostles (and to us):

In a little while you will no longer see Me, and again
after a short while you will see Me . . . because I go
to my Father. . . .

But I will see you again and [then] your hearts will
rejoice, and no one can take from you your joy.[12]
Jn 16:16, 17, 22

In that day of the Spirit's coming to earth there would
be every cause for rejoicing and for continuous praise, for
Satan would be finally worsted, with the victory of the
Cross complete. This supernatural joy then, is the Joy of
the Spirit.

Recently, we witnessed the Spirit bring the gift of His
joy in the midst of cruel circumstances. Mary and George
Greenfield are an attractive couple who began attending
our Monday night church fellowship group in Delray
Beach, Florida. There they received the Baptism of the
Spirit.

Six days after that event their only daughter Patty (a
college sophomore) was abducted during a holdup of the
Cumberland Farms Dairy Store where she worked.

By the next day hundreds of people were praying for

Patty's safety. Yet some of us who attempted to pray for Patty's safe return (including her parents) experienced a check or block, something that was puzzling and hard to interpret at the time.

On the following Monday night (two days after Patty's disappearance) during the singing of "Amazing Grace," George Greenfield's tears began flowing. At that moment, George knew that his daughter was with the Lord. Along with the news came a strong assurance that even poured itself into words, "Don't cry, Dad. I'm okay."

Two days later Patty's body was found by a local detective. Subsequently, police arrested two young men who confessed to the killing.

When a sheriff's detective, an FBI agent, and the Greenfields' minister came together to tell them the sad news, they found the Greenfields' attitude astonishing: they already knew and had been prepared. Though these parents did not understand the "why" of the senseless murder any better than any of us, and while they grieved for their lovely daughter, there was total calmness and no bitterness toward the killers. The newspaper reporters swarming over the case were at a loss to explain the inner strength and sense of victory in the Greenfields—qualities they had never before encountered in such circumstances.

When my husband and I telephoned George and Mary from Evergreen Farm in Virginia where we had gone for the summer, the Greenfields ministered to us over the phone.

Those who attended the memorial service for Patty will never forget the power and beauty and, yes, the shining joy of the Lord that was present. One person described the service as a paean of deeply-felt praise!

Others over the centuries have groped for words to explain the Spirit's gift of joy. Here is how Dr. R. A. Torrey put it after the very sudden death of his lovely, intelligent little nine-year-old daughter Elizabeth from diphtheria:

The next morning . . . as I passed the corner of Chestnut Street and LaSalle Avenue, I could contain my grief no longer. . . . I cried aloud: "Oh, Elizabeth! Elizabeth!" And just then the fountain that I had in my heart broke forth with such power as I think I have never experienced before, and it was the most joyful moment that I have ever known in my life.[13]

How then, do we get the Spirit's joy? Recognize t
more likely to come not when things are going w
whenever we are faced with adversity or problems.
our opportunity to claim part of our inheritance as a child
of the King.

In order to do that, we have to allow Jesus to give us *His perspective on our situation*. Illness, ill will, accidents, poverty, injustice, broken homes are still with us because in our world there is still much mop-up work left from Satan's wreckage. Once a Christian asks for and receives the gift of the Spirit, he has enlisted in the mop-up crew. Then he will be the target not only for his share of the difficulties that are a part of our humanness ("In the world, you *have* tribulation . . ."[14]) but also those special darts Satan reserves for all Spirit warriors. The special darts were exactly what the first Christians were up against. Jn 16:33

Jesus' perspective also includes the long view. Our human view is myopic because it is so self-centered. He insists that we see ourselves as one tiny link in a long line of God's men and women enlisted in the mopping-up process and looking forward not only to a celestial city, but to a time when earth itself will become the kingdom of God ruled by Him, the victorious Christ.

So what is your problem? No matter how bad it is, claim Jesus' own perspective, His own joy in the midst of it. Then really open yourself to that joy and be ready to receive the surprise of your life.

HELPFUL READING: Acts 16:19–34

HIS WORD FOR YOU: Jesus always triumphs.
  But thanks be to God, who in Christ always leads us in triumph.
  (II Corinthians 2:14, RSV)

PRAYER: *Lord, You and I know that I am facing some difficult circumstances in my life, especially my concern about _____. As I ask for Your perspective and Your thoughts on this problem, I begin to see that worry and fretting and taking thought on all the negatives is not being the realistic pragmatist I had thought. In fact, You are telling me that when I wallow in "what-ifs" and discouragement and self-pity, I am ignoring You altogether.*
  As I turn to You, Lord, at this moment and spread this

grief-problem out before You, I hear You say, "There's nothing here I can't handle. Why are you so troubled?"

Your joy shines through Your words, Lord. Let Your joy be mine too. I open my heart to it. Amen.

2 *Faith*

*Now faith is the assurance (the confirmation, the title-deed)
of the things [we] hope for, being the proof of things [we]
do not see and the conviction of their reality—faith perceiving as real fact what is not revealed to the senses.*

(Hebrews 11:1, AMPLIFIED)

The call to faith is all over the New Testament. We are
told that "without faith it is impossible to please" God.[1] Heb. 11:6
Nor can we receive anything from God or get anywhere in Heb
the Christian life without faith. And in one of the greatest
blank-check promises Jesus left us, He pinned everything
to faith:

And whatever you ask in prayer, you will receive, if
you have faith.[2] Mt 21:22

Yet there is a sense in which this imperativeness of faith
simply discourages us. For most of us sense that we *do*
have doubts; we lack the total knowing and assurance that
is faith.

So what is this faith required of us?

We are told that faith is

The substance of things hoped for, the evidence of
things not seen.[3] Heb 11:1

The word "substance" suggests an object—physical
property—while the original word in the Greek carries the
sense of action. Therefore, this might be better translated,

133

Faith is the substantiating of things hoped for.

How do I substantiate something or make it real in my experience? My rock garden at Evergreen Farm in Virginia is a perfect spot for the delightful flower, impatiens. There in that partially shaded spot, the eye-ravishing clumps of pink and cerise and salmon spread and thrive.

Were I blind, those beautiful colors would still be there on the hillside, but I would lack the faculty to verify for myself the pink and the cerise and the salmon.

Even so, our human problem is this: so long as we are in these bodies, we lack the equipment to substantiate divine facts. Our five natural senses are useless in the world of spirit.

In this impasse, faith comes to our rescue. God has ordained it so that faith is the one faculty capable of bridging the chasm between our limiting humanness and God's real world of spirit. Faith then, becomes our inner spirit's eyes, ears, touch, even wisdom and understanding. Only over this bridge of faith can God's real facts about the particular blessings we need out of God's rich storehouse be so substantiated to you and me personally that they become real in our experience.

Yet the fact of those gifts and blessings I need out of God's storehouse[4] did not spring into being at that point in time when I first realized them. They have been there waiting for me all along, just as the colorful clumps of impatiens have all along been there in the rock garden. Were I without sight to verify the impatiens, then neither my skepticism nor unbelief about the plants, nor my belief, would affect the fact that the flowers *are* there.

Even so, the fact of God's supply for me was solidly there, was a fact all along. That is why faith always has to be in the present (denoting completed action), as contrasted with hope which is always in the future.

It was this "presentness" of faith that Jesus was teaching us when He said:

So I tell you, whatever you pray for and ask, believe you have got it, and you shall have it.[5]

So how do you and I get faith—like that? Most of us Christians have tried a variety of ways: rebuking doubts, repeating affirmations, reading Scripture and claiming particular promises, sharing the faith-building experiences of others through the printed or the spoken word.

All of these have value. Yet there is a better way. For it would be possible to use all the faith-building techniques imaginable and still bypass a direct confrontation with the Person of Jesus. Nothing is so important in His eyes as each of us establishing and then activating a personal relationship with Him.

Thus Jesus requires that I come directly to Him to get the faith I need for the substantiating of divine facts to my natural mind. This substantiating *is* revelation, and revelation is the Helper's assigned work in our world.[6]

Seeking such revelation means that in relation to any prayer need, I go to Jesus and ask, "Lord, speak to me about this. What do You want to tell me about it? Lord, pull aside the veil of flesh and give me a peep into the world of spirit. Let me see this situation through Your eyes. What would please You about it? I await Your word on this."

At this point, I am not asking for a change in outward circumstances, just for that inner revelation. Then I wait and listen and watch.

When that insight is given—Jesus' very personal word to me—then faith, "the substantiating of things not seen," automatically follows. And in the wake of that quiet knowing (that "perceiving as real fact what is not revealed to the senses"),[7] external events change. Faith has wrought the miracle of answered prayer.

Our friend Jamie Buckingham tells of such a miracle in his life. At age thirteen he had overheard a nocturnal conversation from his parents' bedroom praising his brother Clay, "I'm so proud of Clay. He's the finest son we have."

The oversensitive Jamie interpreted this, "I love Clay more than I love Jamie." Twenty-five years later Jamie was still struggling with the door slammed shut that night between him and his mother. So resolutely had the door been slammed and padlocked, so deep was the unforgiveness that it had affected Jamie's relationship with all women.

Jamie did not know then to ask for God's revelation on the closed-door problem between him and his mother. In this case, one day the Helper stepped in and graciously gave the insight anyway:

"Let me show you something about those kinds of doors. . . . None of them are real. Once a door like that is bathed in the blood of my son Jesus, it disintegrates. True, it may look as if it is still there, but it's only in your imagination. I have set you free."[8]

This revelation resulted in knowing that his prayer of twenty-five years was answered. The problem was solved. It remained only for Jamie to live out in actions his love for his mother. That turned out to be easy. The word of revelation was correct: there was simply no barrier or problem there.

Only—he needed not have waited twenty-five years. The rich and beautiful answer was there all along.

HELPFUL READING: Matthew 8:5–13; Romans 1:16, 17

HIS WORD FOR YOU: God's storehouse contains everything I need.

Blessing . . . be to the God and Father of our Lord Jesus Christ, the Messiah, Who has blessed us in Christ with every spiritual (Holy Spirit-given) blessing in the heavenly realm!

(Ephesians 1:3, AMPLIFIED)

PRAYER: *Lord, I have been troubled about this situation with _____. My distress about it nags at my mind. Now, Lord, I lay this situation out before You and ask You to speak to me about it. Is there a revelation You can give me? I would like to see this with Your eyes, Lord, so I ask You to take the veil off mine.*

By faith, I thank You ahead of time for Your insight and Your instruction as to how You want me to pray.

I await Your word, Lord. Amen.

3 *Love*

God's love has been poured out in our hearts through the Holy Spirit. . . .

(Romans 5:5, AMPLIFIED)

As soon as we are old enough to enter a Sunday School room, we are taught the simple but powerful words,

"Jesus loves me! this I know,
For the Bible tells me so—"[1]

Certainly a most basic teaching of the Christian faith is this sure knowing of the Master's love for each one of us.

There is a better way, though. Knowing of Christ's love through Scripture is head knowledge. Yet my awareness of His love for me must be more than head knowledge before it warms my heart, touches my emotions, and brings me to my knees in grateful adoration.

Perhaps the greatest distance any of us ever has to travel is that long trek between the head and the heart. Just so, the love of Jesus is something that I must *experience,* and only the Holy Spirit can make me feel that great, tender love.

When the Holy Spirit does pour His love into our hearts like that, how do we respond? How do we, in turn, express our love for Him?

In as many different ways as there are varieties of human beings. . . .

By taking our first steps toward understanding of what

real praise is, we learn that prayer can be adoration of Him, not just asking for things.

We begin to sing and praise Him with our voices in hymn and anthem and simple choruses, even as the Psalmist David did so long ago.

We express our love by lavishing the alabaster box of ointment on Jesus' feet, as Mary did.

Brother Andrew[2] of Holland did this too. He gave all the clothes in his suitcase to his Christian brothers in Cuba who were suffering severe economic persecution. And just before the plane took off for the Netherlands, Andrew took the shoes off his feet and handed them out the plane door to a minister in need of shoes.

We express love too by finding the practicable working out of Jesus' "If a man loves me, he will keep my word."[3] I have a friend who has accepted this injunction literally. For her, the touchstone of every action she takes is simply, "My Lord, what decision in this matter would most please You?"

The young author, Ann Kiemel,[4] goes on a love mission three days each week. Mondays, Tuesdays, and Wednesdays are the days she gives her time, her strength, and her substance to the people in her cosmopolitan Boston waterfront neighborhood—the street sweepers, the waitresses, the delivery boys, the secretaries, the housewives, the janitor of her building. Always, her message is that she has a great Lord and that He loves her so much that He has sent her to tell the waitress or the janitor or the secretary that Jesus loves them too.

For always and always, Jesus' question "Do you love Me?" or "Lovest thou Me more than these?" is followed by His "Then feed my sheep" . . . "Feed my lambs."[5] It is a love that we cannot keep to ourselves. If we do, it withers and dies.

This love is not something we can manufacture in ourselves. The motive power to share His love by sharing the essence of *us* with others in true spirit-to-spirit communication has to be a work wrought in us by the Spirit. Only the Spirit can kindle His fire in our cold hearts.

Sarah Van Wade discovered this when faced with the fact that David, her alcoholic ex-husband, had stopped drinking, had accepted the Lord, and wanted to remarry her and be a father again to their four children. Her first reaction was, "I'd rather die than be married again to David. How could I live with a man I loathe?"

But Sarah had no peace about this. Since she had come to depend completely on the Lord to help her rear four children and provide income through writing, she knew her attitude displeased Him. In a fit of despair, she lay on her bed weeping and praying. "Please, Lord, I'll do anything for You. Don't ask me to go back to David. The children and I are so happy here."

Then Sarah suddenly realized she had told a lie. She was content with her new life as a writer, but the children were not. They had accepted the divorce, but they were not happy without their father. After another storm of tears, Sarah gave in.

"Okay, Lord, I'll see David. I can't stand him for the way he hurt us, but I'll be willing to do what is right. Since I have total deadness for him, You would have to love him through me."

Sarah's willingness to be an instrument for the Lord's love was the key to the reuniting of this family, a story memorably told in their book *Second Chance*.[6] To Sarah's surprise David had really changed. There was a new gentleness in him and a new strength. The Helper not only gave Sarah the gift of a fresh love for her husband which she thought she could never have, but created a new spirit of love in a family where before there had been only bitterness and hatred.

Before Pentecost Peter and James and John and the other apostles had plenty of head knowledge about Jesus. They had fresh, intimate, precious memories of three years with Him. They were as well informed of what Jesus had taught as men could be. They loved Him too.

Yet they were fearful men, frozen into immobility, hiding behind closed and locked doors, incapable of sharing their Master at all, or of feeding any of His lambs lost in a pagan world. They were uninspired men, their inner spirits like the bedraggled sails of their fishing craft hanging limp and motionless on a windless sea—going nowhere.

Until—until the wind of the Spirit filled those sails, billowing them out with such vigor that thenceforward the apostles were not only inspired men, but sent-out, driven men. Surely there is no higher drama anywhere than to look at the Before-After pictures of Jesus' apostles. And this same Before-After drama is what the Spirit wants to recreate in us today.

No wonder we dare not do without the Spirit's work in our lives!

HELPFUL READING: John 21:1–25

HIS WORD FOR YOU: The giving love of God for us.
He who did not withhold or spare [even] His own Son but gave Him up for us all, will He not also with Him freely and graciously give us all [other] things?
          (Romans 8:32, AMPLIFIED)

PRAYER: *Lord, I confess that I have been long on head knowledge of You and woefully deficient in heart knowledge. I have loved You intellectually, but not with the warmth of my heart's adoration. I had not realized, Lord, that Your being loved freely and spontaneously by the creatures You have made is important to You. I had not understood that this is what worship is!*

Lord, I want to love You like that. I ask the Spirit now to be my Teacher. I ask Him to do the work in me, to kindle that kind of fire in my heart. Praise You, Lord. I do love You! Amen.

4 *Vitality*

It is the spirit that gives life, the flesh is of no avail. . . .
(John 6:63, RSV)

Food, vitamins, sleep, rest, relaxation, fresh air, exercise are not the only media of physical restoration. There is another—that of a minute-by-minute supply of vitality and strength given by the Holy Spirit.

We are told that

> . . . if the Spirit of him that raised up Jesus from the dead dwell in you, he . . . shall also quicken your mortal bodies by His Spirit that dwelleth in you.[1] *Ro 8:11*

This is just another facet of our helplessness and of His adequacy. For us to experience this quickening, there must be a reliance on His strength rather than on our own natural vitality.

Dr. A. B. Simpson was a famous New York clergyman whose life roughly spanned the nineteenth century. Always frail physically, while still in his twenties he developed serious heart trouble. Speaking at even three services a week—two on Sunday, one on Wednesday—was excruciatingly hard for him.

Then at thirty-seven, Dr. Simpson's damaged heart was healed by Jesus, a healing verified by the doctors. Thereafter his pastoral, evangelistic, and literary work increased manyfold. Yet always for the rest of his life, he was conscious that he was "drawing his vitality from a directly supernatural source."

141

During the first three years after Dr. Simpson's heart was healed, he kept count and found that he had preached more than a thousand sermons and often held twenty meetings a week. As he put it:

> On a day of double labor I will often be conscious at the close, of double vigor. . . . Nor is this a paroxysm of excitement to be followed by a reaction, for the next day comes with equal freshness. . . . This is nothing less than "the life of Christ manifested in my mortal flesh."[2]

Dr. Simpson founded the still-flourishing Christian and Missionary Alliance and steadily, until his death at seventy-six, turned out prodigious quantities of creative work.

This same physical restoration has also been the secret of the vitality of the beloved Dutch Christian Corrie ten Boom.

During World War II in the Dutch village of Haarlem, the ten Boom family courageously hid a succession of Jews and helped them to escape the Nazis. The entire family was eventually hauled off to Ravensbruck Concentration Camp. Corrie was the only member of her family to survive the long imprisonment.

My husband and I were guests at her eighty-fourth birthday dinner in Miami some time ago. Corrie was still sharp of mind, keen of wit, and as active as ever. For some years she has had angina. Yet when these pains and heart spasms come on her, she goes off by herself to be alone with her Father. Quietly, she waits for Him, knowing He will either take her to be with Him or fill her cup with vitality for more service.

What has come year after year is nothing less than the life of the Spirit transmuted into even the cells and tissues of her body.

HELPFUL READING: II Corinthians 4:6–16

HIS WORD FOR YOU: Life flows from His Presence.
For thus saith the Lord God, the Holy One of Israel: In returning and rest shall ye be saved; in quietness and in confidence shall be your strength. . . .
(Isaiah 30:15, KJV)

PRAYER: *Lord, I would claim the promise of Your Word that Your own life "is manifested in our mortal flesh." I begin to understand that when the Spirit is moving, He adds energy. So I ask now for that quickening power to revitalize each cell of my body. Take away all fatigue. I open myself to receive Your newness of life. Thank you that I will begin to see life with fresh, clear eyes. In Thy power alone, I make this prayer. Amen.*

5 Healing

*So I say to you, Ask and keep on asking, and it shall be
given you. . . .*

*And these attesting signs will accompany those who believe:
in My name . . . they will lay their hands on the sick, and
they will get well.*

(Luke 11:9; Mark 16:17, 18, AMPLIFIED)

I am a very slow learner spiritually. Sometimes it takes
me years to grasp a lesson the Helper is trying to teach me.
Thus I have long pondered why I was not instantly healed
of my lung disease by Jesus' presence in my bedroom that
September night in 1943. That was definitely the turning
point in my illness; from that night there was steady improvement. Yet to many Christians the slow-return-to-
health route does not seem to honor the Lord as much as
dramatic instantaneous healing.

I also asked myself: did an instantaneous or a gradual
healing hinge solely on the level of my own faith? This is a
theology of healing often taught. Yet to believe this places
a burden of guilt on the sick person. The sufferer is already
oppressed by disease; he does not need the added burden of
guilt.

In our time the Helper is now giving us quite a different
explanation: many authentic healings through prayer are a
gradual process rather than a one-time miracle. The complete healing thus takes time and persistently repeated
prayer work. And this slower timing, by the way, is consis-
tent with all normal processes of the body, as well as of
everything in nature.

144

Interestingly, the Helper is currently bring[...]
to the attention of a number of people scattered[...]
Church at large and not necessarily in contact wi[...]
another. Thus the Reverend Tommy Tyson, evangel[...]
teacher from North Carolina, has stumbled upon what he
calls "the soaking prayer." This means that the person
being prayed for is gently bathed in the prayer-atmosphere
for a considerable time. In this case, those praying conceive
of Jesus' life and power as pouring steadily into the
affected area.

Another is Father Francis MacNutt,[1] active for ten
years in the Catholic Charismatic Renewal. He now asks
for a frank appraisal of the results for those prayed for. . . .
Is the pain gone? Is there movement in the affected part of
the body? Is there some or much improvement? From
many such experiences Father MacNutt's best rough summary is that after prayer 75 percent feel demonstrable results. Of that total, 50 percent feel improvement but the
need of further healing.

Teenager Bunni Determan was one who needed persistence in prayer. Bunni had to wear a neck brace because of
severe scoliosis, which is an S-shaped curvature of the
spine. In June 1975, after a group including Father Mac-
Nutt and Bunni's mother (a professional nurse), prayed
with the girl for about ten minutes, some improvement
could be seen. Encouraged, they continued the soaking
prayer for two more hours. By then most of the curvature
at the top of the spine had straightened out.

At this point in his healing work, Father MacNutt often
has to withdraw, and the patient's family and friends in a
local prayer group take over the prayer-work. Thus everyone concerned becomes involved in a growing and learning
experience. With Bunni the healing has continued as her
mother and teenage friends have continued to pray. The
girl is now out of the neck brace and her spine is about 90
percent straight, despite the fact that the medical prognosis
on scoliosis is usually progressive deterioration.

If the soaking prayer seems costly in time and effort
(and it is), a prayer-effort of eight or ten hours for someone like Bunni compares very favorably with the medical
effort of weeks and even months spent in hospitals, the
outlay of thousands of dollars, the pain and trauma of
operations, long series of X-ray or cobalt tretaments, plus
medication that goes on and on.

ever expected five or ten minutes of
ng. Or why any of us have accepted
ught that to pray more than once for
ck of faith.

the opposite. In two separate parable-
le commends dogged perseverance. (See
pful Reading that follows.)

t us the example of the blind man for
whom had to pray twice.[2] After laying His hands on the man's eyes and praying, Jesus asked, "Do you see anything?"

The man's reply was, "Yes—something. But people look queer, like—well, trees walking around."

> Then He put His hands on his eyes again, and the man looked intently [that is, fixed his eyes on definite objects], and he was restored, and saw everything distinctly—even what was at a distance.[3]

Asking questions like "Do you see anything now?" and looking for results actually stimulates faith. When Father MacNutt marked Bunni's spinal S-curvature in red ink, and all those praying could see a noticeable straightening after ten minutes of prayer—even if only a little—everyone was jubilant. Faith then sprang forth to undergird the group for more praying.

The joyous news is that we do not need to wait for the special mission of the healing evangelist. God wants all His people to believe in His goodwill for health and to step out and experiment in prayer. He wants to use all of us.

In early summer 1977 I had a telephone call from an Episcopal priest, the Rev. James Monroe, of Fort Lauderdale, Florida. Danny, the five-month-old baby son of a young couple in his church, had been in a Miami hospital since birth. Only eleven pounds, he could not breathe outside of the oxygen tent. He was being fed intravenously. The fear was that lack of oxygen might have caused brain damage and possibly destroyed his eyesight.

The child's parents were believers and had come to Jim seeking help. He had prayed with them but Danny was not better. Jim Monroe wanted so much to help. Did I have any suggestions?

"Have you anointed the baby with oil and laid hands on him as you prayed?" I asked.

"No, I haven't. Only prayed with Danny's parents. Strange—why didn't I think of anointing with oil? I'll *do* it!"

Six weeks later I received this happy report:

I am delighted to tell you that little Danny is doing marvelously. After I talked with you, his mother and I went together to the hospital. I gave him unction for healing. Since that time he has steadily grown strong. On this past Thursday he breathed normally without oxygen for the first time in his life. He has begun to take food normally in small amounts without tube feeding. His eyesight which we feared to be seriously impaired now seems normal and his little muscles are gaining strength daily. Soon he will be home.

Danny's a *beautiful* baby—big blue eyes, medium brown hair. We give thanks to God daily for exercising His healing power.

The priest added that he was going to persist in prayer for Danny that God would also heal the little boy's memories of those difficult months.

Then I knew that the Helper had been pointing Jim Monroe to persistence in prayer along with the rest of us. Surely, here is one of the keys to the new breakthrough in healing we have been seeking.

HELPFUL READING: Luke 11:5–13; 18:1–8

HIS WORD FOR YOU: He will turn troubles into highways.

He who believes in Him . . . shall never be disappointed or put to shame.

(I Peter 2:6, AMPLIFIED)

PRAYER: *Lord, I think of _____ who is in dire need of Your healing power. Surely, my concern is but a crumb off the loaf of Your encircling love and concern. Yet I confess, Lord Jesus, that I have been content to pray for _____ in private and have never yet gone in person as Your feet and hands and voice with Your promise of healing.*

For so long I have hidden behind my unworthiness and my small faith. I see now that You are asking me not to measure or weigh my faith, just to step out on what I have.

Thank You for this message that Your strength and Your power go with even Your humblest disciples. Since there is added power in agreement in prayer, show us now those You have chosen to go with me to _____. And Lord, grant now as we go that encouragement and improvement in _____'s situation that will signify Your blessing.

You are still the Healer, Lord Jesus; we are only the instruments in Your hands. We praise You that all power in heaven and in earth is still Yours today. Amen.

6 Peace

My peace I give to you; not as the world gives do I give to you.

And the peace of God, which passes all understanding, will keep your hearts and your minds in Christ Jesus.
(John 14:27; Philippians 4:7, RSV)

The peace that Jesus gives us through the Comforter is not dependent on any outside circumstances. It is given right in the midst of great activity or stress or trouble or grief while the storm rages all around us.

Peter Marshall was fond of describing God's peace with a favorite story. . . . At one time a famous artists' association announced a contest. All pictures entered in the competition were to depict "peace." The winner would be awarded a large sum of money.

Paintings of all sorts were submitted. There were serene pastoral scenes; placid lakes; an intimate cottage scene, cheerful and snug before a cozy fireplace; untrammeled vistas of freshly fallen snow; a painting of a tranquil, windless dawn in muted opalescent colors.

But the painting selected by the judges for the first prize was very different from all the others. It depicted the height of a raging storm. Trees bent low under lashing wind and driving rain. Lightning zigzagged across a lowering, threatening sky. In the center of the fury the artist had painted a bird's nest in the crotch of a gigantic tree. There a mother bird spread her wings over her little brood, waiting serene and unruffled until the storm would pass. The painting was entitled very simply, *Peace.*

"That," Peter would point out, "is a perfect picture of the peace God has promised us."

So many have experienced this gift of the peace that "passes all understanding." . . . The young preacher, Malcolm Smith, was in Manhattan's Sloan Kettering Hospital being prepared for surgery early the next morning. Physicians had diagnosed the bleeding mole on his back as deadly melanoma—a malignant tumor.

That evening a strange nurse appeared in the ward. "I've seen many people die," she told Malcolm Smith, "but I've never seen a preacher die." She was half-smiling, half-sneering. "I've always wanted to see if they really believe what they preach. What does it feel like to be dying, preacher?" And she turned on her heel and left.

The taunting words kept ringing in Malcolm's ears. . . . "What does it feel like to be dying, preacher?"

Then a male nurse came in to shave all of Malcolm's chest and back. As he realized how extensive the surgery was to be, terror rose to stick in his throat and engulf him in waves. But let Malcolm himself tell it . . .

The terror screamed, "You prayed and you weren't healed." The thought mocked me. Fear surged and receded like an ocean tide. And like the incoming tide, it always came closer, never withdrawing quite as far as before.

Suddenly a thought came clearly through the tumultuous, encroaching fears: *You have been promised the peace of God under all circumstances. Claim what is yours.*

Malcolm knew that the Lord had spoken. Immediately, he climbed out of bed and headed for the bathroom, the only place where there was any privacy. There he sank to his knees on the cold tile floor.

Instantly, he felt overwhelmed by the love of God and the greatness of God. He felt no need of pleading or begging. Instead, praise and worship of God for being Who He Is poured out in a torrent. And the praise was followed by the glorious gift of God's peace. All fear was gone, evaporated. Malcolm slept soundly that night.

After the surgery the next day the doctors returned their verdict: the wart had indeed been malignant, so they had also removed the lymph glands. Radium therapy was being planned.

Yet two days later a puzzled doctor announced to Malcolm that analysis of the lymph glands had proved them free of cancer. "Somehow there's been a mistaken diagnosis." The doctor appeared to be embarrassed. "Almost never happens. Anyway, you're in fine health and we need this bed. You can go home now."[1]

It is not possible for any of us to go through life without encountering some crises that spawn emotions we cannot handle on our own. But we have to *know* about our inheritance as a child of the King in order to be able to claim it. "The peace that passes all understanding" is an especially precious part of that inheritance that not a one of us can do without.

HELPFUL READING: Galatians 5:22–24; Philippians 4:4–8

HIS WORD FOR YOU: The Lord has heard and will deliver.

> *Though I walk in the midst of trouble, You will revive me: You will stretch forth Your hand against the wrath of my enemies, and Your right hand will save me.*
> (Psalm 138:7, AMPLIFIED)

PRAYER: *Lord Jesus, even in these lovely days sometimes I find fear in my heart as I wonder what the next few years will bring. We are living in uncertain, troubled times. How I thank You that Your gift of peace does not depend on circumstances at all.*

I praise You that You have hidden me, Your child, as in the hollow of Your hand, and that the Father's great hand rests over all. I praise You that this citadel of rest and peace is mine whenever I need it and ask You for it. Let me feel this, Lord, so that my spirit relaxes into Your peace. Thank You, Lord, thank You. Amen.

7 Other Tongues

*And they were all filled with the Holy Spirit—they began
to speak in foreign tongues, as the Spirit enabled them to
express themselves.*

(Acts 2:4, MOFFATT)

One of the Helper's characteristics is that He is practical
and pragmatic. We expect just the opposite. "Holy Ghost"
or "Holy Spirit" sounds so other-worldly, so high-flown.

But the Helper's mission during this era of the Spirit is
to us earthly creatures still in the flesh. We are the ones
who are always pretending that we are more "spiritual"
than we are. The Helper, on His side, deals with us in a
rational, realistic, down-to-earth manner.

One of Jesus' specific commands for this era of the Spirit
was to "go into all the world and preach the gospel to
every creature."[1] The Helper knew that the minute the
disciples took this seriously, they would run into language
barriers. Jerusalem was more of a melting pot than some
areas of New York City are today. So with his usual prac-
ticality, the Helper moved to solve that problem.

In the miracle that followed on the day of Pentecost,[2]
fourteen separate languages and dialects are mentioned as
being used by these unlettered men and women, with other
dialects flicked at. This was the gift of "other tongues."
Later, another aspect of the same mystery would appear—
a heavenly language, sometimes not a known one, yet always subject to the speaker's will.[3]

Certainly more controversy has swirled around this gift
than any of the others. The common misconception that
the gift of tongues is ecstatic, unarticulated babbling is not

152

the New Testament position. Rather, Paul seems to assume that any heavenly language always would have an interpretation, if we had faith to believe that and could but make connection with an interpreter. Therefore his advice about use of the gift in private and his warnings against misuse of the gift in public are based on this premise.[4] *I Cor. 14*

Everything Paul has to say about tongues reflects a common-sense, balanced view. On the one hand, he refuses to give this one gift undue emphasis or importance; on the other, he will not reject it.

Then do we have authenticated instances of "other tongues" in our time? Yes, we do. Many instances. Of those I know, here is a true incident told me by my friend Betty Malz of Pasadena, Texas. Betty is the tall, attractive author of that memorable life-after-death experience, *My Glimpse of Eternity*.

A considerable portion of her childhood was spent in Attica, Indiana. Betty's father ministered in the little frame Rosedale Church. Rosedale saw many astonishing answers to prayer and many of God's miraculous gifts bestowed. As for instance, what happened some years ago one hot summer evening to Betty's quiet, shy mother, Fern Perkins, who scarcely ever raised her voice in church.

The congregation was suffering with the heat, so the church's double doors opening onto a little porch were wide open to catch any breath of air stirring. In the middle of the service two things happened simultaneously. . . .

Inside the church Betty's mother was suddenly told by the inner Voice to stand up and pray in her heavenly language. Fern Perkins' natural reserve and reticence about such a thing were swept aside by a compulsive inner pressure: she *had* to obey.

As she did, outside the church an elderly Greek coal miner, his miner's cap and lantern still on his head, was walking by the church as he headed home from work. This man was in deep discouragement. Coal mining had been the only job he could find. The pay was small and the hours long. He never saw the light of day: he went to work before sunrise and returned after dark. To add to his discouragement and loneliness, he had found no one in the community who could understand his Greek, and he spoke little English.

As he plodded along past the Rosedale Church, suddenly through the open doors he heard a woman's voice speaking

perfect Greek. At last! At last someone with whom he
could talk!

Impulsívely, the man sped into the church, spotted the
woman from whose lips still came that beautiful modern
Greek. Ignoring the stares of the worshipers, he began
excitedly jabbering to Mrs. Perkins in his native tongue. Of
course Betty's mother could not understand a word he was
saying.

By now the church was in an uproar. Gradually, the
truth dawned on both sides. It was a miracle straight out of
the Book of the Acts because the miner himself was able,
haltingly, to translate the message that was manna to his
spirit. As Betty recalls, it was something like this . . .

God loves you. God has a purpose for your life and
for your family. He has the power to forgive sins, to
bring you joy and hope and loving purpose. He *will*
give you a path to travel that will bring joy and peace
to you and to those you love so dearly.

When the man realized that his new friend did not naturally speak Greek, and that God had taken hold of her
tongue and spoken this through her, he dropped to his
knees, and with tears pouring down his cheeks, began
praising God. Then and there the miner gave his life to
Jesus.

From then on, he and his family not only attended
Rosedale Church regularly and made a host of friends
there, but several other families were drawn into the
church because of this one miracle of the Helper's gift of
"other tongues."

HELPFUL READING: Acts 2:4–21

HIS WORD FOR YOU: The rock like characteristics of
the Kingdom.
   And all His decrees and precepts are sure—fixed, estab-
   lished, and trustworthy.
      They stand fast and are established for ever and ever,
   and are done in [absolute] truth and uprightness.
         (Psalm 111:7, 8, AMPLIFIED)

PRAYER: *Lord, I ask You today for the Helper's gift of*
present-tense faith because past-tense faith suffices not at

all for the needs of today. I see that I can be thoroughly "orthodox" and agree that the early Church long ago experienced Your power in miraculous ways, yet have this affect my life not at all.

With my mind, I know that "You are the same yesterday, today and forever."[5] Then why do I keep limiting You today? I ask you to break this barrier in me—now. Give me an open, expectant will and heart that goes out to meet You, still the miracle-working Lord, right now.

I worship You, Lord Jesus. I praise You that You are still the Lord of heaven and of earth, with all power. Amen.

Heb 13:8

8 *Miracles*

Holding the form of religion but denying the power of it. . . .

All power is given unto Me [Jesus] in heaven and in earth.
(II Timothy 3:5, RSV; Matthew 28:18, KJV)

What does Timothy mean when he refers to "holding the form of religion but denying the power . . ."?

It is time to be plain about this. The Holy Spirit insists upon taking us into the realm of the miraculous. Unless we can follow Him into this world of miracles there is no way that we can receive the fullness of the Spirit.

The Bible from Genesis to Revelation is peppered with examples of the supernatural intervention of God. By that is meant an act invading our time-space planet over and beyond what we humans have come to expect in the concept of nature as a "closed system." By "closed system" we mean natural law observable and definable, rigid, rather than being pliable and regulated by the sovereign God.

Here is the dictionary definition of "miracle":

An event or effect in the physical world beyond or out of the ordinary course of things, deviating from the known courses of nature.[1]

As for Jesus' attitude toward the supernatural, His is an insistent bugle call to the faith that there is no human need His Father cannot meet: no disease, no matter how hideous or far advanced, no cruel circumstance His Father cannot handle.

In Jesus' total trust in His Father we can see at least three strands: first, "Power belongeth to God."[2] Jesus believed this so totally that over and over He moved out to stake His life and His entire reputation on the validity of this fact.

This is perfectly illustrated in the story of Jairus, ruler of a synagogue, who approached Jesus begging Him to come to his home and heal his desperately ill twelve-year-old daughter. At that moment a messenger arrived to tell the sad news, "Your daughter is dead: do not weary and trouble the Teacher any further."[3] Lk. 8:49

Would any of us have gone to the dead girl to pray for her recovery? Scarcely! To do so would make us look like a fool, or worse, insane.

And our human reasoning always gets in the way in a situation like this: "What if prayers aren't answered? Won't that destroy the faith of the girl's parents and many other people too?"

Obviously, no such doubts entered Jesus' thinking. He went straight on to Jairus' house, took the child's cold limp hand in His, and with calm audacity said, "Child, get up!"

And she did open her eyes and get up, to the stunned amazement of everybody.

The second strand of Jesus' faith and trust in the Father was His insistence on God as having all love. Over and over, He compared God to the most loving human father we know or can imagine. Anything that ordinary human love longs to bestow—taking away pain, restoring sanity, pouring out joyous gifts, providing food and housing or any other material resource needed, directing us to the right job, giving ideas and inspiration and wisdom, restoring severed relationships, preventing premature death—all this and more, Jesus insisted, the Father's love wants to give us.

But the first two strands would not be enough to help us, if God had not left to Himself the liberty of stooping to intervene in human affairs. This third strand is that He does reach down to answer our prayers. Were He, in fact, rigidly encased and bound by the natural laws of the universe He Himself had called into being, then the miracles as recorded in the gospel narrations could never have happened.

Quite the contrary, Jesus knew perfectly well about natural law—seedtime and harvest, famines, tempests, hunger and starvation, disease and death. All this made no one whit of difference to Him. Very simply, Jesus' faith was that His Father was over and above all natural law; was omnipotent over anything in earth or in heaven. could and would stoop to relieve human need unhampered by any rival power. *Acts 1:22*

Then when we leave the Gospels and go on to the Acts the disciples gathered at Pentecost and became, to a person, "witnesses to His resurrection."[4] Not all the one hundred twenty who gathered in the Upper Room had been present in the garden on resurrection morning. That did not matter. The important thing was that they accepted unequivocally the bodily resurrection of their Lord from the dead. He had been dead. He was now alive. Not just spiritually. Not just a ghost. Physically alive, as they themselves were alive.

This acceptance changed their viewpoint about everything. In the face of this stupendous miracle-fact, any other miracle was possible and probable. Then God could do *anything!* Believing *that*, they were prepared to let the Spirit use them to stand the Roman world on its head.

And we too must believe in the resurrection as those first century men and women did, with no effort to spiritualize it or explain it away. Practically speaking, this means that we make a clear-cut decision of our wills no longer to duck the impossible situations in our orbit. Like Jesus on the way to Jairus' little daughter, we too, knowing full well our helplessness, must walk right on, opening ourselves and the "impossible" circumstances to the miracle-working power of the Spirit.

When we dare this, the promise still stands:

Every place upon which the sole of your foot shall tread, that I have given you....[5] *Joshua 1:3*

Forever and forever, this is the Helper's challenge.

HELPFUL READING: Mark 5:22–43; Luke 8:41—56

HIS WORD FOR YOU: God's giving knows no limit.
If God is for us, who can be against us? The God who did not spare his own Son but gave him up for us all surely He will give us everything besides!
(Romans 8:31, 32, MOFFATT)

PRAYER: *Lord Jesus, I see human need all around me. I can't help thinking of _____ and _____ . They are desperate. Only a miracle can handle their situations.*

Suddenly, I have a new viewpoint of miracle-working faith, Lord. It does not mean that I have any power or instant piety of my own. Or that You have handed me a big slug of confidence or emotional euphoria that I might mistakenly call faith.

What faith does mean is that I'm willing to be used of You for _____ and _____; and that I believe You when You tell me that You Yourself, the risen and glorified Lord, will be present and in me when I go to _____ and _____ to bring the power of God to earth exactly as You did long ago.

As I go forth to these friends, the work will be Yours, not mine. The results will be Yours too.

Lord, guide me now. Shall I pick up the phone? Tell me the first step.

Thank You, Lord. Amen.

Part Six

The Helper
and the Church

1 Has My Church the Spirit?

And He has put all things under His feet and has appointed Him the universal and supreme Head of the church. . . .

Which is His body, the fullness of Him who fills all in all— for in that body lives the full measure of Him who makes everything complete. . . .

(Ephesians 1:22, 23, AMPLIFIED)

In the post-resurrection days before Jesus' ascension to the right hand of the Father, He charged His disciples not to try to form a church or to attempt any work for Him until they had received the Spirit. They were to wait in Jerusalem until they were endued with power, commissioned for service.[1] *LK. 24. 46-49*

The reason was obvious. Here were one hundred twenty disciples—mostly uneducated fishermen and tradesmen, along with some humble women—so filled with fear of the Jewish hierarchy on the one hand, and the power of Rome on the other, that they hid behind locked doors.

Looking at them cowering there, we might wonder whether Christianity had any chance at all. Poor, terrified, broken crutches they seemed! What chance would such unlettered and untalented folk have against entrenched Jewish tradition and the screaming eagles of Rome's might?

But Jesus had a plan. The one hundred twenty were to become Christ's Body on earth. That Body came into being at Pentecost. Thus Pentecost is the birthday of the Christian Church.

From that day the Holy Spirit was given an altogether new office. Into His hands was placed the administration of every detail of the life of the Church. The plan was that from Jesus' ascension into heaven until His return to earth, He would be our Paraclete in heaven, there to be the "head over all things for the church."[2] The Holy Spirit would be our Paraclete on earth to administer and order the "building up of the body of Christ"—the Church.[3] *Eph 4:12*

That is why, apart from the Spirit, the Church of Christ has no viable life. Any Christian church that ignores the Spirit is an apostate church. Moreover, the *full* blessings of Pentecost can only be experienced by the fellowship of believers in the Church, never by the solitary Christian.

In explaining this to the Ephesian Christians, Paul did not say that the Church is *like* a body, but that it *is* the Body of Christ. And that "the full measure of Him who makes everything complete lives only in that Body."[4] *Eph 1:2*

Practically, this means that not only in worship, but in prayer and in service and ministry to others, we cannot get along without one another. For instance, Jesus often gives pieces of the insights needed for prevailing prayer to several members of the Body. As for ministry, He would not normally give all of the gifts of the Spirit to one individual.

As for the how of Christian maturity, there can be no growth or deeper life for any of us separated from our fellow-Christians. Individualism and our old life of independence are no good, Jesus tells us, simply because we will die if we continue that way: no branch can live unless attached to the Vine. And the Vine has not a single branch, but many branches.

Once we see the necessity of this kind of Christian fellowship, our next task is to find the right Body of Christ for us. As given us in Scripture, here are some questions to help point the way. . . .

Where does my church stand in regard to the Holy Spirit?

Am I and my fellow church members really functioning as Christ's Body on earth?

Does the Person of Jesus occupy a central and preeminent place in the preaching and life of my church, as over against emphasis on loyalty to the church as an organizational and denominational entity?[5] *Col 1:18*

Does my church recognize in any way the offices that the Spirit would like to fill, such as pastors, preachers, teachers, evangelists, prophets, healers, miracle-workers, helpers, administrators?[6] *Eph 4:8-12*
I Co 12:28, 29

(Isa 61:6   I Pe 2:5   Rev 1:6)

To what extent is my church a practicing body of the "priesthood of all believers?" (Or are we still mostly a spectator church relying on the professional church staff?)[7]

Are strangers who come to my church impressed with the atmosphere of joy and praise and genuine worship? Does the singing reflect that joy?[8]   Ro. 14:17

Is there deep caring for one another, as shown by the sharing of material resources as well as spiritual experiences? Are there any needy in my church whose necessities are not being met?[9]   Acts 4:32-35

Are any of the sick being healed?[10]   I Co. 4:20

Are we in our church seeing lives being steadily turned upside down, reclaimed for Jesus? Are there recovered alcoholics? Broken homes mended? Estranged children reconciled? Drug addicts and mental patients cured? Lost people who find a new purpose in life?[11]   II Co 5:17 I Pe. 1:23

Are we in our church experiencing power over sin in our daily lives? For instance, are we progressively shedding ego hang-ups, hurt feelings, selfishness, lack of love? Are we being convicted of the sin of unbelief by the Spirit?[12]   Jn 16:8-11
Acts 2:37

HELPFUL READING: Revelation 3:13–22

HIS WORD FOR YOU: Mountains of obstacles melt before him.

> *Then he said to me, This is the word of the Lord to Zerubbabel, saying: Not by might nor by power, but by my Spirit, says the Lord of hosts.*
>
> *For who are you, O great mountain of [human obstacles]?*
>
> (Zechariah 4:6, 7, AMPLIFIED)

PRAYER: *Lord Jesus, I confess disappointment, sometimes even disgust about my church. If the infighting in churches, between Christian groups, and in Christendom generally sickens me, how heinous must all this lack of love be to You, Lord.*

Yet I know that discouragement or disgust is not right. Nor is giving up on the Church. For she is Your Body on earth. And no matter how stained her garments, we have Your promise that "the gates of hell shall not prevail against her," and that finally, the Church will be presented to You in glorious apparel.

Meanwhile, Lord, I make two requests. Please straighten out my attitude about my church. Make it right before You. And show me, Lord, a first constructive step that I can take on behalf of my church, Your Body, in this place.

I await Your direction, Lord. Thank You! Amen.

2 *He Brings Reconciliation*

Now I beseech you, brethren . . . that there be no divisions among you; but that ye be perfectly joined together in the same mind and in the same judgment.

God, who . . . gave us the ministry of reconciliation. . . .
    (I Corinthians 1:10, KJV; II Corinthians 5:18, RSV)

What is the Church? It is not the building. That we know. Nor is it an organizational or denominational structure.

The New Testament definition of the Church is the Greek word *ekklesia*[1] with two facets of meaning: "the called out ones" and "those called together."

There is also Paul's vivid analogy or synonym for the word *Church:* "the body of Christ."[2]

So a group of the called-out ones who have been tapped by the Lord to live and work and pray and minister together, comprise the Church, the Body of Christ in any given place. To these have been entrusted one of the passions of Jesus' heart, His ministry of reconciliation.

Since the Helper will always faithfully reflect Jesus' own Spirit and viewpoint, His most fervent desire would also be the Helper's. We can be certain then, that wherever the Spirit is allowed to enter, He will always be indefatigably working at the mending and re-fusing of broken relationships.

So where do Christ's followers stand with this matter of reconciliation?

In the first-century Church immediately after Pentecost,

Jesus' prayer for oneness and unity was gloriously answered:

> And the multitude of them that believed were of one
> heart and of one soul: neither said any of them that
> ought of the things which he possessed was his own;
> but they had all things common.[3] *Acts 4:32*

Here was no forced sharing as in state socialism or communism. Rather it was altogether voluntary, based simply on the caring of these men and women for one another.

And the oneness today? We have to concede that the fragmentation of Christ's Church is a scandal. The Church's divisions and cliques and infighting are one of the biggest stumbling blocks to the acceptance of Christianity of those outside the Church. Our factions and our resentments, one to the other, dishonor our Lord as nothing else can.

Not only that, the separateness and divisions drive the Helper away. Quietly, He simply departs. Our beautiful church building is left to us, along with our tranquil, perfect worship forms. The church organizational machinery carries on as usual—the church boards, the regular meetings of this and that. Everything appears to be intact: we will, we think, go out "as at other times before" when all the while we have no notion of the tragic truth: "we wist not that the Lord was departed from us."[4] *Paraphrase of Judges 16:20*

Yet there are bright spots in our day too. The Spirit is on the move with, as always, incredible results.

My husband Leonard and I have watched at close range a modern example of reconciliation which has come out of Washington's Watergate scandal. Obviously, Watergate produced intense distrust, violent resentment and anger—a climate of hostility and hatred involving many in the nation's capital. Among them, former Senator Harold Hughes, a political liberal and such a vigorous critic of President Nixon that he was a top man on that administration's enemies list. Thus Hughes became a particular target for Chuck Colson, Nixon's "hatchet man."

Colson thought Hughes a menace to the nation because of his violent and outspoken opposition to Nixon policies.

Hughes thought Colson the epitome of evil as the leader of the White House gang. In politics, Chuck Colson stood for everything that Harold Hughes hated.

Then in an incisive way the Holy Spirit moved into Chuck's life, cleansing him, changing him, bringing him to his knees.

Years before, Hughes had already had the same experience. It had happened at a time when Harold had been contemplating suicide because of despair over his anger about life and his drunkenness. Jesus had been Rescuer and Savior to him in every sense.

Then came the dramatic moment when Harold and Chuck were brought together through an intermediary, Doug Coe, head of the Washington Fellowship Group.[5] In order to take a little of the heat off, Doug had decided to make it a quiet evening with wives at the home of Al Quie, Minnesota Republican Congressman. Doug had also invited a former Democratic Congressman from Texas, Graham Purcell and his wife, Nancy. The setting was the Quies' paneled family room with the group gathered around a mammoth brick fireplace.

In the midst of the others, Colson and Hughes were rather like two boxers waiting in their separate corners for the sparring to begin. Then abruptly Harold began the action. "Chuck, they tell me you've had an encounter with Jesus Christ. Would you tell us about it?"

So Chuck described what had happened that memorable summer night near Boston when a life-long barrier between him and his God had been broken down. To his surprise, Colson felt no embarrassment in talking about this, the most intimate experience of his life, yet he was supremely conscious of his inadequacy.

Here is Chuck Colson's own description[6] of what happened as the spirit in Hughes heard his spirit testify of Jesus Christ:

> For a moment there was silence. Harold, whose face had been enigmatic while I talked, suddenly lifted both hands in the air and brought them down hard on his knees. "That's all I need to know. Chuck, you have accepted Jesus and He has forgiven you. I do the same. I love you now as my brother in Christ. I will stand with you, defend you anywhere, and trust you with anything I have."
>
> I was overwhelmed, so astonished in fact, that I could only utter a feeble, "Thank you." In all my life

no one had ever been so warm and loving to me outside of my family. And now it was coming from a man
who had loathed me for years and whom I had known
for barely two hours.

Then we were all on our knees—all nine of us—
praying aloud together. . . .

These men became close friends, part of an intimate
Christian fellowship, though even today they have differing
points of view politically.

Later on would come another night at Fellowship House
in Washington, D.C., when the Helper brought together in
one room four incredibly disparate individuals—Eldridge
Cleaver, once a prime target of the Nixon administration
as well as of the Justice Department as Black Panther
leader; the former head of the Ku Klux Klan (pledged to
keep blacks in total submission through terror tactics);
Colson; and Hughes. After years of rebellion, all four men
had made dramatic surrenders to Jesus. Where in all the
world could four such unlikely candidates for Christian
fellowship have been found? Yet that night saw the four
praying together. This is the reconciliation that the Spirit
brings!

As we witness the miracle of it we realize that true
oneness of mind, heart, and spirit is not something we can
program or manipulate; it is the priceless gift of the Spirit.
Then let us not deceive ourselves that it can be achieved by
shaking hands or hugging a neighboring worshiper at a
scheduled point in a church service. Or by making small
talk with someone over a cup of punch in the so-called
fellowship hour.

These can be good beginnings, but the true reconciliation Jesus is asking of us is not fellowship game-playing: it
means patient listening to another's point of view in an
effort to understand; painful apology perhaps, and in the
end it always involves sharing life deeply on a continuing
basis with our own *ekklesia*—those who have been called
together by the Spirit Himself.

HELPFUL READING: Matthew 5:24; 18:15; Ephesians
4:1–8; 23–32

HIS WORD FOR YOU: God's people claim their inheritance of peace.

*Let Christ's peace be arbiter in your hearts: to this peace
you were called as members of a single body. And be
filled with gratitude. Let the message of Christ dwell
among you in all its richness. Instruct and admonish
each other with the utmost wisdom.*

(Colossians 3:15, NEB)

PRAYER: *Lord, I need You in my home and in my
church. Without You, we are separate human beings going
our separate ways.*

*This day come into the heart of each of us who lives here
and into every room in this house. Only with Your presence
will it be a home.*

*And Lord, my church is very needy. We go through the
motions of worship, we brush one another politely on the
way out. But what a sad parody this is of the oneness You
want for us!*

*Lord, let Your ministry of reconciliation now begin in
me. Tell me now where I can begin to erase misunderstand-
ings. What can I do today to affirm another human being,
to encourage someone discouraged? Let me be a bridge
between You, Lord Jesus, and one of Your children who is
hurting. And take away from me the selfishness that I like
to call sensitivity.*

*We need You in this place, Lord. Abide with us today.
Amen.*

3 He Cleanses the Body of Christ

Therefore, putting away falsehood, let everyone speak the truth with his neighbor, for we are members one of another.

And do not grieve the Holy Spirit of God. . . .
(Ephesians 4:25, 30, RSV)

Each of us has faced the dilemma: a fellow-Christian or a member of our family is "overtaken in a fault." Perhaps there is moral slippage, or anger and unfairness to a child or a marriage partner, or a slide towards alcoholism, or a vicious tongue causing rifts in the office or the church. We care deeply about the erring one. What are we to do? What is *our* responsibility?

In past centuries the local church often disciplined such a one. I have been astonished to read in old nineteenth-century records (for instance, of Washington, D.C.'s New York Avenue Presbyterian Church) of a drunkard or an adulterer having been actually summoned before the Session for questioning and corrective discipline.

Currently, in certain Christian groups there is something of a return to this group correction. Passages like I Corinthians 5:1–6 and Titus 3:1–10 have convinced us that bad leaven really can contaminate the whole; that the Spirit of *Holiness* cannot tolerate evil that invites Satan to enter a family unit or a church; that therefore we *do* have a responsibility not to shut our eyes to sin; that ignoring wrongdoing never deals with the problems caused by evil.

172

Thus some of these groups try to convict the wrongdoer by "light" or truth sessions with, in some instances, severe spiritual and psychological damage. Two clergymen in one such group were plunged into nervous breakdowns from which they were many months recovering. In another instance the head of one community has taken it upon himself to point out the sins of members and to administer not only correction but punishment—with disastrous results.

Surely, the lesson here is the truth Jesus made clear in His Last Supper talk: it is the Spirit's province, and His alone, to convict of sin. "When *He* comes, *He* will convince the world of sin. . . ."[1] Jn 16:8

When we try it on our own, we are seeking to usurp the Helper's place. The result of attempting in the flesh to convict another of sin is wreckage—defensiveness, anger, estrangement, loss of self-worth, defeatism, depression—whereas, when the Spirit does this corrective work, it is "good" hurt, the kind that leaves no damage, that never plunges us into despair or hopelessness but is always healing in the end.

Do we then have no part or responsibility in this? Yes, we do. A close look at Jesus' words immediately preceding the passage already mentioned . . .

But if I depart, I will send him *unto you.*

followed by

When He comes, he will convince *the world* of sin. . . .[2] Jn 16:7, 8

shows us that God does intend to use human beings as channels for the Helper in the conviction of sin—as also He uses us with intercessory prayer, with the teaching and preaching ministries, with healing, and all the rest. To get to the needy world all around us, the Spirit has to use those whose bodies are already His living temples. His plan then is to work through the Spirit-baptized believer individually as well as through the Church Body.

Over and over we see the working out of this plan in the Acts' narrative. The Spirit used Simon Peter's Pentecost sermon to bring three thousand to conviction of sin.[3] Acts 2:14, 41 Again Peter was used in the case of Ananias and Sapphira.[4] Acts 5:3, 9? Philip was the Spirit's human conduit for the correction of Simon the sorcerer.[5] Later we see the Spirit working Acts 8:9-24 through Paul to correct Simon Peter himself,[6] and so on.

Jesus Himself had laid a solid base for such correction: "If your brother sins, rebuke him,"[7] and "Go and tell him his fault."[8] Mt. 18:15   Lk. 17:3

Yet this remains a difficult assignment for which we desperately need the Spirit's help. Most of us either want to shirk altogether being used by the Helper for any correcting or disciplining work, or else we become judgmental and try it on our own without love. Continually, we need to beware of our incorrigible human blindness to our own faults as contrasted with the way we see other people's faults as if under a giant magnifying glass.

When we do begin to accept responsibility for others around us, what safeguards should we establish?

(1) We have to be convicted by the Helper of our own sin first before He can use us for others. Especially of our sin-nature and of the root sin of unbelief.

(2) We have to be willing to be used for the Helper's convicting work, and tell Him so. It helps to remind ourselves often that Jesus' purpose is never to condemn men, but always to free them for happiness and rich fruit-bearing for Him.

(3) Many a Christian down the centuries has found that the Spirit cannot use him for the conviction of another until he is willing to become involved in that other's life, to do anything or make any sacrifice. We need to face up to this. This is love in action and it can be costly.

(4) We need to be sure that a loving relationship exists between us and the person to be corrected. If there is already anger and resentment, the correction will only tend to make the situation worse.

How can we know whether we are moving with God's love, or in fleshly judgment? Tests to apply here are a tender grief for the guilty one, with a jealousy for God's honor before men and a deep strong faith in Jesus' power of deliverance in the wrong situation.

(5) We need to undergird the correction first with prayer, asking the Spirit to do the work. This is all-important. We need to pray also for the Spirit's own love and gentleness, and to ask close friends to be in prayer while we are administering the correction to another person.

We have only to brush guidelines like these to realize that our real trouble is not caring enough and not taking time for the prayer that would link us to Him who can solve all problems.

HELPFUL READING: Matthew 18:15–22; I Thessalonians 5:12–22

HIS WORD FOR YOU: How to deal with those who wrong us.

> *Beloved, never avenge yourself, but leave it to the wrath of God; for it is written, "Vengeance is mine, I will repay, says the Lord."*
>
> (Romans 12:19, RSV)

PRAYER: *Lord, how can I who am still so flawed be used for the correction of anyone else? I ask You to save me from the cowardice that makes me unwilling to be used at all, and from a holier-than-thou spirit that would attempt any part of this on my own strength.*

I do see the point of correction: By our sin, we have given Satan ground on which to stand and we bring more wreckage to our lives, to our homes, our businesses and our churches. Thank You for the Spirit's power in cleaning up the ground and expelling Satan.

You alone, Lord, can make me usable to You for this work. Make me a willing instrument in Your hands. In Your strong name, I pray. Amen.

4 *He Brings Unity*

*I do not pray for these only, but also for those who believe
in me through their word, that they may all be one; even
as thou, Father, art in me, and I in thee, that they also may
be in us, so that the world may believe that thou hast sent
me.*

*Now the company of those who believed were of one heart
and soul. . . .*

(John 17:20, 21; Acts 4:32, RSV)

Jesus' Last Supper talk with His eleven apostles was
over. Well He knew what lay just ahead for Him—
ignominious betrayal, rejection by His own people, ruth-
lessly cruel mauling and manhandling followed by a linger-
ing death.

Yet just before He resolutely walked out over the Brook
Kidron to the Garden of Gethsemane, He paused for what
we know as His High Priestly Prayer.[1] Jesus' thoughts
were not on Himself or the physical cruelties just ahead;
His concern was for us who would "come after."

So much was this oneness of heart and mind and spirit
Jesus' passion that He reiterated this petition four separate
times. He was leaving the world, He said, to return to the
glory of heaven. He knew that all would be lost without
that unity. Therefore, into the hands of the Helper—the
Emissary to earth he was about to send—He placed the
responsibility for the carrying out of this prayer request.

When we look at the fragmentation of the organized
Church today, all might seem to be lost. So many denomi-

nations and splinter groups! Scarcely a local church without infighting and factions. Little real Christian unity even yet between racial groups—blacks and whites, or differing nationalities, or disparate economic classes.

Such minuscule progress towards unity dramatizes for us what does *not* work. Making laws will not do it. Education does not bring unity either. Not even rallies, marches, strikes, and blatant propaganda can effect true oneness. In the United States black-white segregation has seen two decades of laws and education and every external device, but even yet we make painfully slow progress.

So how is the answer to Jesus' High Priestly Prayer to come about? Scripture makes it plain that the Holy Spirit is the only real unifying agent in our world. This was one of the first discoveries of the one hundred twenty men and women after Pentecost. As though to dramatize His unifying mission, the Helper first wiped out language barriers.[2] Economic differences and possessiveness were then dissolved.[3] National and religious taboos and theological exclusiveness were in turn leveled by the Spirit.[4]

And in the midst of these miracles

> The company of those who believed were of one heart and one soul....[5]

and

> They partook of food with glad and generous hearts, praising God and having favor with all the people.[6]

The same kind of miracles take place in our time wherever we will allow the Helper to work. It was a thrilling experience to sit at the center of the Arrowhead Stadium in Kansas City, Missouri, at the 1977 Conference on Charismatic Renewal and see 50,000 pairs of arms raised, 50,000 voices crying, "Jesus is Lord"—Christians—Catholic, Messianic Jew and Protestant from every major denomination worshipping in unity.

South Africa, torn asunder by the starkest racial disunity on our planet, was represented by Archbishop Bill Burnett, by the Reverend Charles Gordon, and others. These men told us of the wildfire spread of the Spirit in Africa today where 25 percent of the white Anglican and Presbyterian clergy are now Spirit-baptized. They see this move of the Spirit as Africa's only hope for survival without total holocaust and a Communist takeover.

Apart from the Spirit, *apartheid* (Afrikaans for "separateness") rules in South Africa. There, whites are only 17 percent of the total population. The blacks must live in separate townships (such as Soweto near Johannesburg) where less than one-third of the blacks' homes have electric lights; less than one-tenth, running water. Seething hatred is rampant.

Yet the Spirit can dissolve even such formidable barriers as these. Charles Gordon, minister of a church in Durban, told how the Helper directed them to send word to the blacks that they would be welcome at the regular weeknight services held in white homes.

In discussing this prospect, someone remarked to Mrs. Gordon, "And probably, a big black Spirit-filled man will come up and hug you." Charles was astonished to see the blood drain from his wife's face. With an ashen face, she questioned, "You aren't serious, are you?"

"I'm being partly facetious, I suppose," the friend replied, "but it really *could* happen, you know."

"The strange part is," Charles told us, "my wife attended a very liberal college, and she has extremely broad views on issues like race. Yet she had no control over that inherited, built-in reaction."

After the meeting was in full swing the following week, a knock came on the door and two black men entered. All seats were taken. After a hushed, tense moment, two young men rose to offer the visitors their seats.

At the close of the meeting, one of the blacks, a tall, burly man, crossed the room and exuberantly lifted Mrs. Gordon off the floor, praising God as he hugged her.

"And do you know," Charles told us wonderingly, "my wife seemed to be completely composed. Isn't that amazing!"

Before leaving for their own townships, the visitors told the assembled group, "Word came to our compound that there are people who love even blacks. We came tonight to find out if it was true. And it is!"

The passion of Jesus' heart for oneness will be fulfilled— but only by the Helper's work in our world. After all, this oneness is of man's inner spirit, and only the Spirit can melt our hard hearts and our stubborn insistence that we are right and everyone else wrong. Only the Spirit can change the climate of our inner spirit so that we are able to receive and welcome a dissentient human being into our hearts.

HELPFUL READING: Ephesians 2:14–22

HIS WORD FOR YOU: Jesus always opens prison doors.
Now the Lord is the Spirit, and where the Spirit of the Lord is, there is liberty—emancipation from bondage, freedom.

(II Corinthians 3:17, AMPLIFIED)

PRAYER: *Lord Jesus, show me any wrong attitude in me that would impede the answer to Your passionate prayer for unity and oneness.*

I think of _____ and _____ who, I know, bear grudges and resentment against me. They are Your children too and You love them as much as You love me.

As You know, Lord, all my efforts at righting these situations have failed. Now I see why only the Helper can convict any of us humans at the heart level and bring about reconciliation.

So now, O Holy Spirit, I turn this task over to You. As You work in _____ 's heart and _____ 's, keep me alert and sensitive so that when the moment of reconciliation comes, I will gladly go more than my half of the way to meet my friends.

By faith, I praise You for this new unity ahead. Thank You, Lord. Amen.

5 Channels for His Power

*Truly, truly, I say to you, he who believes in me will also
do the works that I do; and greater works than these will
he do, because I go to the Father.*

(John 14:12, RSV)

Acts 3:1-8 ; 5:15, 16   8:6-7 ; 14:8-10

This is one of the most staggering promises Jesus ever
made. When we consider the works He did—curing the
sick, healing leprosy, opening blind eyes and deaf ears,
restoring crippled limbs, curing palsy and arthritis, returning the violently insane to normalcy, yes, and even raising
the dead—then was Jesus seriously promising that we—
you and I—would not only do these same works, but even
greater works? Could He be serious?

As we read the Acts we find that His early apostles did
take this preposterous promise at face value and proceeded
to act upon it. No doubt they discussed among themselves
precisely what Jesus had meant by *greater* works. But in
the meantime they *were* healing the sick and the crippled.[1]
They *did* raise the dead.[2] Acts 9:36-41 ; 20:9-12

Those first-century disciples were able to be channels for
such amazing miracles because they took seriously the all-
important link between Jesus' "works" and theirs that most
of us are missing today: the Holy Spirit was the connection
between the humanity of Jesus and the Father.

After their Master's resurrection, they understood finally
His divinity: He really was "the only-begotten Son of the
Father." But all along, these men who had walked the
roads of Palestine with Him had realized the reality of
Jesus' humanity in a way that we have still not grasped.

180

Heb. 4:15

He was real flesh and blood. They watched Him get hungry and thirsty and often very weary from the jostling, demanding crowds. Then too, they knew that "He was tempted in every way as we are. . . ."[3] Nor were these temptations easier for Jesus to resist than they are for us, for Satan always shrewdly sees to it that only the higher reaches of subtlety and finesse are presented to more spiritual persons. We could admire from a distance a Lord who could not sin; we can give our heart's devotion only to a Savior who understands our every weakness because He has been there too.

The Apostle Paul would express this true humanity of his Lord in unforgettable words:

> Though he was divine by nature, he . . . emptied himself by taking the nature of a servant.[4]

Phil. 2:6, 7

How real this "emptying" was, Jesus sought again and again to impress upon His followers. He was insistent that they grasp this all-important fact that was to be the bridge from His life to ours. . . .

> I am able to do nothing from Myself—independently, of My own accord; but as I am taught by God. . . .[5]

Jn 5:30

> I do nothing from Myself—of My own accord, or on My own authority—but I say [exactly] what My Father has taught Me.[6]

Jn 8:28, 29

> Whatever I speak, I am saying [exactly] what my Father has told Me to say and in accordance with His instructions.[7]

Jn 12:50

> The Father that dwelleth in me, he doeth the works.[8]

Jn 14:10

He was saying, "I have no power in Myself. The emptying is complete. Believe Me, I am only a channel for my Father's power. In exactly the same way (after I have ascended to My Father, after I am no longer the empty servant but the glorified Lord and the crowned Christ), then you also will be channels for My power. It was the

Spirit who made it possible for Me to do my Father's works. It is the same Spirit (whom I will send to you) who will make it possible for you to do My works."

Surely *that* is why He was looking forward to an era of greater works. We do not yet know all that this means, but one thing is clear: as the number of Spirit-baptized Christians multiplies, eventually there can be many thousands doing His works.

Then why are we not doing them? It is noteworthy that one of the first serious heresies of the infant Church of the late first century and early second century was Docetism—the denial of the real humanity of Jesus. The fact that miracles began to die out about that time has usually been attributed to declining faith. True, no doubt. But behind the anemic faith lies a significant fact. As the years went on, Christians no longer saw Jesus as their "Brother" as the early disciples had. Increasingly, He became a figure sculpted in marble, painted in oils with a gilded halo, encased in stained-glass windows.

By being in awe of such an inaccessible Jesus, they sought to honor Him, but in also dropping out the Holy Spirit, the third Person of the Trinity—that all-important link between His humanity and ours—they really dishonored Him.

The promise is still there for us—that we can "do greater works." The Spirit as Teacher is eager to lead us on and out into new dimensions, yes, even of the supernatural. Do we have the faith to believe and the courage to act?

HELPFUL READING: Mark 16:15–20; Acts 1:4–11

HIS WORD FOR YOU: God never changes.
> *For God's gifts and His call are irrevocable—He never withdraws them once they are given, and He does not change His mind about those to whom He gives His grace or to whom He sends His call.*
> (Romans 11:29, AMPLIFIED)

PRAYER: *Lord Jesus, I begin to see that while You walked the earth in human flesh, the Spirit taught You and was Your link with the Father, just as now He wants to teach me and be my link with You. I understand better now in what sense You really are my Brother.*

*How I thank You, Lord, that I don't have to be "worthy"
of any of this. How could I be? Instead, what I ask for is
the willingness to empty myself of me even as You were
willing to be emptied. I know it's a daring prayer, Lord.
Give me the courage for it. Amen.*

Docetism — that Christ
was a mere phantom,
or maybe a celestial being.
(not human)

Notes

Foreword
1. Joel 2:28, 29.
2. Luke 1:15.
3. A. B. Simpson, *The Gospel of Healing* (Harrisburg, Pa.: Christian Publications, Inc., 1915), pp. 178, 75.
4. Joshua 1:3 (KJV).

I. Introducing the Helper

Chapter 1 Who Is the Helper?
1. Romans 8:27.
2. I Corinthians 2:10, 11.
3. I Corinthians 12:11.
4. Acts 20:28.
5. I Corinthians 12:8–11; Ephesians 4:7–12.
6. John 16:13, 14.

Chapter 2 Why Do I Need the Helper?
1. Acts 1:4 (AMPLIFIED)
2. William R. Moody, *The Life of D. L. Moody* (New York: Fleming H. Revell Co., 1900), pp. 146, 147, 149; and R. A. Torrey, *Why God Used D. L. Moody* (New York: Fleming H. Revell Co., 1923), pp. 51–55.
3. Matthew 5:6.

Chapter 3 Have I Already Received Him?
1. Galatians 3:24.
2. Matthew 11:11 (AMPLIFIED)
3. Luke 11:13.
4. John 15:26.

5. Romans 8:14.
6. Galatians 5:22; James 2:8, 9.
7. Romans 8:26.

Chapter 4 No Need to Be an Orphaned Christian
1. John 16:7.
2. A. B. Simpson, *When the Comforter Came*, (Harrisburg, Pa.: Christian Publications, Inc.).

Chapter 5 Could Anything Be Better Than His Presence?
1. "The Sweet Story of Old," Jemima T. Luke, 1841.
2. John 16:7; 14:17.
3. I John 3:9 (AMPLIFIED).
4. Jeremiah 31:33 (KJV).
5. John 15:5.
6. John 15:1-8.

Chapter 6 The Explosion of Power
1. Acts 1:1-5.
2. This interesting analysis is summarized from James Burns' *Revivals, Their Laws and Leaders* (London: Hodder & Stoughton).
3. Acts 2:37-41.
4. Acts 8:14-17.
5. Acts 19:1-7.
6. Acts 10:44-48.

II. How Do I Receive the Helper?

Chapter 1 Hungering and Thirsting for Something More
1. Revelation 3:15, 16.
2. Luke 18:1-8.
3. Matthew 5:6.
4. John 7:37-39 (RSV).
5. R. A. Torrey, *The Holy Spirit* (New York: Fleming H. Revell Co.), p. 198.
6. Luke 11:9 (AMPLIFIED).

Chapter 2 Accepting Jesus as the Christ
1. John 14:6 (RSV).
2. Acts 4:12 (RSV).
3. Revelation 19:16.
4. Revelation 5:12.
5. Colossians 2:10; Ephesians 3:10; 4:8-10; I Corinthians 15:24.
6. Romans 5:17 (AMPLIFIED).
7. Luke 15:11-32.

8. Luke 15:32 (KJV).
9. Bilquis Sheikh, *I Dared to Call Him Father* (Lincoln, Va.: Chosen Books, 1978).

Chapter 3   Deciding to Obey the Good Shepherd
1. James 2:17–22.
2. Philippians 2:13 (AMPLIFIED).

Chapter 4   Inviting Jesus as the Baptizer
1. John 20:21, 22 (AMPLIFIED).
2. Graham Pulkingham, *Gathered for Power* (Plainfield, N.J.: Logos International, 1972; and New York: Morehouse-Barlow Company, 1972), pp. 75, 76.

Chapter 5   Being Willing to Be Put to Work
1. Acts 1:8.
2. W. H. Daniels, *Moody, His Words, Works, and Wonders*, p. 396.

Chapter 6   Repentance and Baptism: Rising to New Life
1. Acts 2:14–39.
2. Norman P. Grubb, *Rees Howells, Intercessor* (Fort Washington, Pa.: Christian Literature Crusade), pp. 38–40.
3. *Ibid.*, p. 29.
4. I Corinthians 15:50.
5. Romans 6:6 (AMPLIFIED).
6. Romans 6:3 (AMPLIFIED).
7. Ephesians 2:5, 6.
8. Colossians 2:10.

Chapter 7   Accepting God's Grace
1. Galatians 3:1–5.
2. Acts 2:32, 33.
3. Watchman Nee, *The Normal Christian Life* (Fort Washington, Pa.: Christian Literature Crusade, 1964), p. 88.
4. Ephesians 1:20, 21 (RSV).
5. John 14:21.
6. See Devotional, "He Values My Personhood," in Part IV.

III. How the Helper Meets My Everyday Needs

Chapter 1   He Saves Me Time
1. I Corinthians 12:4–10.

Chapter 2　He Guides My Actions
1. Acts 13:3.

Chapter 4　He Is with Me in Everyday Situations
1. John 15:5 (AMPLIFIED).

Chapter 5　He Is My Remembrancer
1. Luke 21:12–15 (RSV).

Chapter 6　He Gives Me New Desires
1. Romans 8:14 (AMPLIFIED).
2. Romans 8:15 (AMPLIFIED).
3. Romans 12:2 (AMPLIFIED).

Chapter 7　He Changes My Undesirable Habit Patterns
1. Galatians 5:22, 23.
2. Luke 2:52 (RSV).

IV. How The Helper Ministers to Me at a Deep Level

Chapter 1　He Convicts Me of Sin
1. Acts 2:23, 37 (RSV).
2. John 3:17 (RSV).
3. Romans 3:23; I John 1:8; John 8:34 (RSV).
4. Luke 4:18.
5. I John 1:9.

Chapter 2　He Values My Personhood
1. Philippians 2:7.
2. Mark 10:21.
3. Ephesians 4:25–32.

Chapter 3　He Teaches Me about Tears
1. Matthew 19:8.
2. Psalm 95:8; Hebrews 3:7–11.
3. Hebrews 3:13; Ephesians 4:17, 30–32.
4. Mark 3:5; 8:17; Romans 2:1–5.
5. Luke 19:41, 42.
6. John 11:34–36.
7. Jamie Buckingham, *Daughter of Destiny* (Plainfield, N.J.: Logos International, 1976), pp. 163–67.

Chapter 4　He Is My Comforter
1. Hannah Whitall Smith, *My Spiritual Autobiography* (New York: Fleming H. Revell Co.) pp. 211, 215, 216 (now out of print).

Chapter 5 He Teaches Me to Pray (I)
1. Luke 11:1 (RSV).
2. John 16:24 (AMPLIFIED).
3. I John 5:14.

Chapter 6 He Teaches Me to Pray (II)
1. I Peter 2:10 (MOFFATT).
2. Ephesians 1:3 (AMPLIFIED).
3. John 5:19 (AMPLIFIED).
4. John 5:30 (AMPLIFIED).

V. The Outpouring of the Helper's Generosity

Chapter 1 Joy
1. Galatians 5:22.
2. Acts 4:3.
3. Acts 5:18, 40.
4. Acts 7:58–60.
5. Acts 8:3.
6. Acts 12:2.
7. Acts 12:3, 4.
8. Acts 16:25 (AMPLIFIED).
9. John 15:11 (AMPLIFIED).
10. Hebrews 12:2 (KJV).
11. Hebrews 1:9 (KJV).
12. John 16:16, 17, 22 (AMPLIFIED).
13. R. A. Torrey, *The Holy Spirit* (New York: Fleming H. Revell Co.), p. 95. For the full story, see pp. 93–95.
14. John 16:33 (RSV).

Chapter 2 Faith
1. Hebrews 11:6 (RSV).
2. Matthew 21:22 (RSV).
3. Hebrews 11:1 (KJV).
4. Ephesians 1:3.
5. Mark 11:24 (MOFFATT).
6. John 14:26; Luke 21:12–15; John 16:14, 15, etc.
7. Hebrews 11:1 (AMPLIFIED).
8. Jamie Buckingham, *Risky Living* (Plainfield, N.J.: Logos International, 1976), pp. 89–91.

Chapter 3 Love
1. Words by Anna Warner; music by William B. Bradbury.
2. Another portion of Brother Andrew's story is told in *God's Smuggler* by Brother Andrew with John and

Elizabeth Sherrill (New York: The New American Library, 1967).

3. John 14:23 (RSV).

4. For more on this author, read *I'm Out to Change My World* by Ann Kiemel (Impact Publishers).

5. John 21:15–18.

6. David and Sarah Van Wade, *Second Chance* (Plainfield, N.J.: Logos International, 1975).

Chapter 4 Vitality

1. Romans 8:11 (KJV).

2. A. B. Simpson, *The Gospel of Healing* (Harrisburg, Pa.: Christian Publications, Inc., 1915), pp. 170, 171.

Chapter 5 Healing

1. Francis MacNutt, *The Power to Heal* (Notre Dame, Ind.: Ave Maria Press, 1977) pp. 39–45.

2. Mark 8:22–26.

3. Mark 8:25 (AMPLIFIED).

Chapter 6 Peace

1. Malcolm Smith, *Turn Your Back on the Problem* (Plainfield, N.J.: Logos International, 1972), pp. 87–89.

Chapter 7 Other Tongues

1. Mark 16:15 (KJV).

2. Acts 2:7–12.

3. Acts 10:44–48; 19:4–7.

4. I Corinthians 14.

5. Hebrews 13:8.

Chapter 8 Miracles

1. *The New Random House Dictionary of the English Language.*

2. Psalm 62:11.

3. Luke 8:49.

4. Acts 1:22.

5. Joshua 1:3 (AMPLIFIED).

VI. The Helper and the Church

Chapter 1 Has My Church the Spirit?

1. Luke 24:46–49.

2. Ephesians 1:22 (RSV).

3. Ephesians 4:12 (RSV).

4. Ephesians 1:23 (AMPLIFIED).

5. Colossians 1:18.
6. Ephesians 4:8–12; I Corinthians 12:28, 29.
7. Isaiah 61:6; I Peter 2:5; Revelation 1:6.
8. Romans 14:17.
9. Acts 4:32–35.
10. I Corinthians 4:20.
11. II Corinthians 5:17; I Peter 1:23.
12. John 16:8–11; Acts 2:37.

Chapter 2 He Brings Reconciliation
1. Acts 5:11.
2. I Corinthians 12:12, 13.
3. Acts 4:32 (KJV).
4. My two-word-change paraphrase of Judges 16:20.
5. My personal knowledge of the situation described here came through Leonard LeSourd's close involvement with Colson in editorial work on the book manuscript of *Born Again* and the friendship with him that has resulted.
6. Charles W. Colson, *Born Again* (Lincoln, Va.: Chosen Books, 1976), p. 150.

Chapter 3 He Cleanses the Body of Christ
1. John 16:8 (RSV).
2. John 16:7, 8.
3. Acts 2:14–41.
4. Acts 5:3, 9.
5. Acts 8:9–24.
6. Galatians 2:11–16.
7. Luke 17:3 (RSV).
8. Matthew 18:15 (RSV).

Chapter 4 He Brings Unity
1. John 17.
2. Acts 2:4–12.
3. Acts 2:44, 45; 4:33, 34.
4. Acts 10; 11:1–18.
5. Acts 4:32 (RSV).
6. Acts 2:46, 47 (RSV).

Chapter 5 Channels for His Power
1. Acts 3:1–8; 5:15, 16; 8:6, 7; 14:8–10.
2. Acts 9:36–41; 20:9–12.
3. Hebrews 4:15.
4. Philippians 2:6, 7 (MOFFATT).
5. John 5:30 (AMPLIFIED).
6. John 8:28, 29 (AMPLIFIED).
7. John 12:50 (AMPLIFIED).
8. John 14:10 (KJV).